EMBERS
—— OF ——
HOPE

When Depression Comes to Church

Bryan Cerrone

ISBN 979-8-89309-123-6 (Paperback)
ISBN 979-8-89309-124-3 (Digital)

Copyright © 2024 Bryan Cerrone
All rights reserved
First Edition

All rights reserved. No part of this publication may be reproduced, distributed, or transmitted in any form or by any means, including photocopying, recording, or other electronic or mechanical methods without the prior written permission of the publisher. For permission requests, solicit the publisher via the address below.

Covenant Books
11661 Hwy 707
Murrells Inlet, SC 29576
www.covenantbooks.com

CONTENTS

Acknowledgments v
Note to Reader vii
Introduction ix

Chapter 1: Elijah (Burnout) 1
Chapter 2: Heman the Ezrahite (Dark Night of the Soul) 14
Chapter 3: Job (Integrity) 31
Chapter 4: Esther (Invisible to Others) 48
Chapter 5: Hannah (Cries of Desperation) 63
Chapter 6: Father of the Demon-Possessed Boy (Belief
            and Unbelief) 76
Chapter 7: Naomi (Facing Uncertainty) 89
Chapter 8: Jeremiah (Remaining Faithful) 100
Chapter 9: Jonah (When Bitterness Festers) 113
Chapter 10: King David (It Can Happen to Anyone) 129

ACKNOWLEDGMENTS

I have so many people to thank when it comes to this book. First, thank you to Victoria, my amazing bride, who has always been there for me and never gave up on me in my weakest moments of life. Thank you for the countless hours you spent listening to me pour out my heart. *I love you.*

I want to thank my dad, Gary Coombs. He came into my life as an eighth grader and became the dad I never had. He also encouraged me to move forth with this book idea and became a huge champion for me.

I want to thank my incredible children because they are an intricate part of my story. They give me so much hope, and I love them more than they could ever imagine.

I want to thank my friend David, who took the time to read through my rough draft and give me his honest thoughts. When I was 80 percent of the way through and took a pause, he was persistent in reminding me to finish. Thank you for your persistence. Thank you for our friendship.

I want to thank Bob and Cyndi Swanson (Dad and Mom) for your listening ears, your encouragement, and your investment in my life on multiple levels.

I want to thank you, the reader, for opening this book. My prayer is that you'll be blessed.

And finally, and most importantly, thank you, Jesus, for not giving up on me. Thank you for loving me in ways that I'm still trying to wrap my head around.

NOTE TO READER

What you are about to read started off as a journal entry. Within four late nights in August 2023, 80 percent of this book was written. Then came a break because life sort of got busy. That happens when you have five wonderful kids and are in full-time ministry. I finally got around to finishing the final 20 percent around the holidays after a persistent daily nudge from my friend, David.

INTRODUCTION

One of the things we don't talk about enough in church and in Christian circles is depression. Sure, we'll allude to it in different ways, but we really don't get into the nitty-gritty of it all. And when we do talk about it, it's sort of surface-level talk. Once the conversation gets a bit uncomfortable, we jump ship or pass the conversation along to someone else who can deal with it in a less public way. After all, if we're honest, we don't really like the types of conversations that burst our me-and-Jesus emotional high, do we?

Depression is very real and can plunge into the lives of Jesus-loving, Spirit-filled Christians at any given moment. It can come when you least expect it. Yes, Spirit-filled Christians can battle depression and still love Jesus. So allow me, with my speedy fingers and "Jesus + Therapy" coffee mug, to be a bit honest and vulnerable with you.

Every Sunday, as a pastor, I look out into the congregation and can see the sadness and loneliness behind the smile, the superb Sunday outfit, and the "I've got my life all together" mentality of family units. To further give credence to this statement, the Sunday morning appearance doesn't quite match the midweek mentoring/counseling reality with those same exact families.

For so long, I've been told that depression and one's faith don't belong together; that it's impossible for the two to be combined. Some will say that if you're depressed then it really means that you're not filled with the Spirit, you're not a true believer, you're not completely surrendered to Jesus, you don't really love Jesus that much, you don't really take the Bible seriously, depression is a manifestation of Satan, and the list goes on.

There have been times when I've been told to just "release" it to God and rise up and move on. I've been told to figure out a way to get over this or to get more faith and everything will be fine. I've been told that the Bible commands us to be thankful in every circumstance (1 Thessalonians 5:18); therefore, just cheer up a bit and be thankful. I've also been told that having depression is being a functional atheist, and what's outward always signals what's really inside. In other words, having depression is like believing in one thing but living in a way that tells others you don't really believe it.

I've been told that it's been long enough sulking in sadness and that I need to get over myself already. I've been told that you can't lead anymore if you're on empty because you've got nothing to give, so this makes you somewhat disqualified. Chances are, you've probably been told some of these things as well. Oh, and isn't it ironic we can make the "disqualified" statement at the same time as saying amen to a sermon about God qualifying the called?

See, this is what's called taking the Bible and using it as a weapon to beat others with. It's also, if we really want to be honest here, spiritual malpractice. I've seen this done so many times under the umbrella of so many topics.

When I went to the doctors some time ago to figure out what was wrong with my body after having multiple nights of intense esophageal pain (actually, for years now), the doctor didn't prescribe for me medicinal purposes that remedies a whole different issue. The doctor didn't take a bunch of random bottles of pills and tell me to take them all and your issues will eventually be taken care of. No, he figured out what was going on and gave a few specific instructions that would help me live a better life. He listened carefully to the problem and carefully prescribed the solution. He wasn't flippant and certainly wasn't careless in his approach with me.

In the same way, there are so many Christians who know a few Bible verses and love to throw them at every single issue without taking into context the verses they are throwing, the people they are throwing them at, and the situations they are throwing them into. These same people will just throw the Bible as a whole to you and say some of the most spiritually insensitive things known to mankind.

This also can happen when one knows the Word of God but not God Himself. Not always, but often.

If I may say, when it comes to depression, churches can be challenging places to seek healing. Not all, but far too many. I am not including this statement out of bitterness. I am including it because it's a reality we need to be aware of and hopefully, one day, we can change this reality. I am burdened by this because I have seen so much church hurt caused in this area. I have seen so many situations that have been handled poorly and this has led people to be pushed to the fringes of society.

I get it, the church isn't perfect and, oftentimes, doesn't have any expertise in this area. Yet at the same time, it doesn't require expertise to treat others as Jesus would. It doesn't take expertise to slow down our programs and minister to hurting individuals. It doesn't take expertise to slow down and walk alongside someone who's going through a lot in life and to just be there for them. A statement I like is this: proximity breeds empathy. If we take the time to get close to others, to hear and understand their stories, and to do life together with them, we'll be better caretakers of those around us.

I'm going to be honest here and take the risk of being vulnerable with you. I hope that, in my transparency and "heart on my sleeve" approach, I can inspire a movement that brings awareness to such a pressing issue. I've experienced depression a handful of times in my life; a couple of those times were while serving in ministry pastorally. One of those times was in 2014, and one was most recently in 2022 going into 2023. This most recent one was really, really dark, and it felt lonely. It felt lonely for a number of reasons.

First, my wife, Victoria, was going through a ton of things in her own life, and I didn't want her to have to deal with me or worry about me. She had enough on her plate. I tried to hide it, but some of it just seeped out. I was so angry at times and felt so selfish in having to be "hit" with depression at the same time when I should have been the strong one for my wife and kids. I was so bitter at the timing of it all. I screamed out to God, "Could you have allowed me to go through this at a different time!"

Second, I'm a pastor, and I've been conditioned to think for many years that pastors and church leaders should never experience depression while in leadership. After all, we are the spiritual leaders with a more direct connection to a holy and majestic God, right? Note the sarcasm. So I hid it. There were times when I just didn't want to do ministry anymore, times when I was confused, times when I was uncertain about what's ahead, and times when I felt like a complete failure. It would take three times as much energy every Sunday morning to just push through and not give any hints that anything was wrong. I mean, we do that very well on Sunday mornings across the board and all over in our American churches.

There were days when all I could do was remain quiet and just respond with an "Everything is fine" comment and attitude when asked what was wrong. Some days, when I thought it might be brighter out, were just filled with unexpected intense storms. There were times when I just didn't even know how to process what was going on inside of me. Like, I don't even know what's wrong to even tell you. I don't want others to say, "Here we go again." Some moments felt very frustrating. I could be on an emotional high one moment and then sink to the lowest the next moment and really couldn't even pinpoint a trigger. How could I be running around and being a goofball with my kids one moment and then sink so low the next moment like someone just killed my dog? This was frustrating to the people around me. It was frustrating to me.

Interestingly enough, as I was working on this most recent paragraph, I came across an Instagram post about Robin Williams. It sparked my curiosity, so I went a little deeper and started to find articles titled "Robin Williams Masked Depression with a Veil of Comedy" and "The Funny Face of Depression."

As you may know, we lost him to suicide in August of 2014. Robin, like many others in comedy and others who have a sense of humor, found comedy and laughter as a defense mechanism. Robin didn't have the greatest relationship with his mother, but he found that his comedy made her laugh and, therefore, drew him closer to her.

We all know Robin as a great comedian and a great actor. When he died, it shocked the world. Behind the smiles, the laughter, the entertainment, was immense pain. I say all this because there's a danger to this stoic society we've created, and the church needs to be a haven that counters this.

Third, I didn't know who to talk to or who to trust. Can I talk to my wife? Yes, but I wanted to protect her too. You know, you would think that things that you've "dealt" with from the past would just remain there, right? You would think that your past is distant enough to not affect you. But what I've found was that the enemy loves to bring things up from the past at the worst possible moments and speak loads of condemnation.

This past year was riddled with intense memories from my past, ranging from the abuse I went through as a child, the turmoil I went through with my grandparents, the stupid decisions I've made growing up, to the memories that life totally sucked at times. I just didn't know who I could talk to that wouldn't turn my confidence against me. I'm confident you know what I'm talking about. We've all confided in people we thought we could trust, and it completely backfired on us. It's a level of hurt experienced that none of us want to go through.

Am I blessed right now? Absolutely. I have a beautiful wife, five incredible children, a ministry calling, a roof over my head, my bills are paid for, and so much more.

So why is it that I felt this way? Why is it that no matter how long or how loud I cried out to God for help that the season just wouldn't go away? Why were they coming at all in the first place? What was wrong with me? Why did I feel like I was failing as a follower of Jesus, as a husband, as a father? Why would God allow me to go through these dark seasons when I've literally signed up to be in His army to serve others? All kinds of questions filled my mind. I decided to go on a journey because this was not the life I wanted to just accept.

I went on a journey because, though I felt a sense of despair, I had faith that all hope wasn't completely lost. This journey started one night as I was sitting alone in front of a campfire.

The air was cool, the fire was raging, and I needed to just sit alone and reflect. I felt defeated. I felt worn. I felt lost. I stared at the fire as the smoke shifted direction every few moments. The sky was on the brink of nighttime and the first bunch of stars twinkled.

I kept staring and just sort of got lost in the moment. And then I saw that there was no raging fire anymore. At that moment, in a very weird way, clouds came in and covered the stars.

As a good former Eagle Scout, I went to get this raging fire back, but to no success. After a few attempts, I sat back in my chair and stared at what appeared to be a small glowing ember. I remember thinking, *If only God could do something with a small glowing ember.* Why? Because that's what I felt I had left in my soul. I couldn't muster up the strength to blow into it and get the fire of passion, meaning, and purpose raging again. I felt so faithless. I felt like I was a loser. I felt that others were on fire for Jesus and here I was with a small, little glowing ember wondering what could possibly be done with that. I felt really angry too. This is not who I am. What happened to the fire and passion and zeal to do crazy things for Jesus? Could it be that Jesus was more interested in healing me than in my performance?

Well, I just sat there in my chair and whispered to the Lord, "I don't know what you can do with a small glowing ember in my soul, but here it is."

I decided to start therapy because I believe you can love Jesus and therapy together. I believe that Jesus uses this process to speak to people, and honestly, I wish everyone would go to therapy before it's "too late." I also started therapy because I had nothing to give. I had nothing to lose by going. Why not go? I had no reason not to go, so I just went. Full disclaimer here: I never wanted to go because I was so scared of what the experience would be like. I had questions. Would I have to relive previous moments to be properly healed? And what if it doesn't work? Well, after years of contemplating getting help, I just stepped outside of the boat and believed that Jesus would grab me by the hand. Here we go.

But more importantly, I turned to the Bible more than ever before. Of course, as a pastor, I'm always reading the Bible, but this time, I wanted to read it with fresh eyes and more devotionally. I wanted to read it to spend time with Jesus; not to take things from it to relay some spiritual messages to the people I was leading. I asked God, "Can you just show me *You*?"

For years, I've studied the Bible professionally. I knew a lot of it, but I asked God to reveal *Himself* to me; not just facts on a page. I didn't want to just know about the God of the Bible; I wanted to know Him personally on a deeper level. I wanted to read the Bible with fresh eyes. I wanted to know if all these heroes of the faith in the Bible escaped the realities of what it means to be human. Well, of course not, but it's funny how we forget that biblical characters like King David, a man after God's own heart, lusted after a married woman, had her husband killed, lost his baby, and wrote Psalms of intense lament. There's so much reality that enveloped that hero who slayed Goliath.

We named one of our sons Elijah after the prophet in the Bible, and I remember a few things about Elijah that I thought it would be a great idea to start off by looking at his story. What was his life like? What were his human experiences outside of calling fire down from heaven, performing the first resurrection in the Bible, outrunning chariots and horses, personally slaughtering a few hundred prophets of Baal, and so forth?

And then, because my mind tends to wander in directions that don't make sense, names began to come to mind of biblical heroes in the Bible who were far from meeting the expectations of today's church people who weaponize the Bible. Like, didn't Jonah want his life to end? Didn't Jeremiah cry nonstop? Didn't Peter feel intense guilt after denying Jesus, which led to Jesus needing to restore him on the beach? Didn't Job wish he would just die in the womb of his mother? Didn't Jesus sweat drops of blood? Didn't Paul have many sleepless nights and experienced anxiety for all the churches that he personally planted?

I think there's something here. Every single one of these biblical heroes would be told to get over yourself by many church folks today, and it's funny that we quote these very same biblical characters to admonish the very people who experienced the same things as the biblical characters quoted! Can you imagine saying, "Elijah, you got to stop being so depressed because you're missing out on so many potential ways the Lord can be using you"? Who of us can even measure our ministry impact with all the things Elijah did?

Depression is at an all-time high right now, and it's wreaking havoc everywhere. I am not a professional when it comes to this area, but I am sharing a portion of my area that I think has a lot to say to those of us who go through these moments and seasons.

There are so many variables when it comes to the reasons we experience depression, and it's important to understand that. Some of it may be emotional, physical, genetic, spiritual, and some of it may be a combination of it all. And though I would argue that the spiritual component envelopes all our seasons of depression, we must understand that it would be completely foolish to just pray all of our problems away. God has gifted individuals in different fields to help remedy some of the struggles we go through. I am very wary when folks tell me that if you just take it all to Jesus and not worry about what the doctor says, it'll be just fine. You've just got to have faith. I tend to brush those people off a bit because it's normally the ones who are on mountaintop journeys saying such things.

Some wisdom and discernment are needed here.

If you or a loved one are experiencing depression, please seek help. I hope my words can speak to you, but please do allow trusted others to walk alongside you in the healing process. I am also urging the churches to please allow spaces where conversations around depression can take place in a safe way. Please allow spaces that are safe and confidential and where we can promise we won't ostracize individuals to a cordoned-off ministry area somewhere away from the main center of ministry. Please talk about this from the pulpit.

Finally, yes, I am a full-time pastor who is willingly and openly going to be vulnerable when it comes to this topic, and I want you to know that Jesus absolutely loves you even in those moments where you struggle to think this is true. Yes, I've lost loved ones who went through depression, and I've lost count of friends and even pastors who succumbed to the destruction of depression. May Jesus carry them in His arms forever.

The people that we've lost to the battle of depression are real people with real stories and real emotions. Whether it's a close friend or family of ours, or it's a celebrity like Chester Bennington, or a pastor like Jarrid Wilson, or a former youth group member, all these precious individuals are those to whom Jesus laid his life down for on the cross. Let's remember that.

Before I delve into our first chapter, let me briefly tell you what my intention is here. My intention is to focus on a major biblical character per chapter. I want to take us through their lives and to uncover their world in which they've battled depression, intense despair, sadness, loneliness, and hopelessness. What do they have to teach us? What precious takeaway is there for us that'll give us some hope? How did God view them, and how did God tend to their souls? How did they bring together their everyday experiences with the hope they knew about God? These are just a few questions I want to take us through. It is my hope that as you read these chapters and read about these biblical characters, you'll not feel alone in your struggles. It is also my hope that you'll be inspired to take even more time to go back to your Bibles and learn more about the lives of these characters.

While there are so many people I could dedicate this book to, a few names stick with me. In no order of importance, I think of my dad, who came into my life and became that important figure for me in the eighth grade. I think of Ariel, the sister of my wife, who sadly passed away after battling depression in 2023 at the age of twenty-six. I think about Mason, my wife's brother, who passed away in 2022 at the precious age of seven. I think about my family who has gone through so much in such a short period. And I think about you who were brave enough to enter this conversation. This book is for you.

It is my prayer that Jesus will do something very special for you and to you on your journey.

Now let's see if we can make sense of this little glowing ember and the possibilities that can arise.

CHAPTER 1

Elijah
(Burnout)

I alluded to some of the great things about Elijah some moments ago, so I won't repeat them at great length, but I do think it's worth remembering that this prophet was one of two people in the Bible who never experienced death. Man, I got so many more questions than answers about that kind of experience, but that's a little fun fact to keep in the reserves of your memory.

Before we jump into his story, let me give you some context, some background so that his story doesn't become confusing for us.

Elijah was a prophet who lived around 900 BCE—that is, about nine hundred years (give or take) prior to when Jesus entered the scene of humanity. He lived during a turbulent time of Israel's history (was there ever not a turbulent time?) and his major ministry impact was during the reign of King Ahab and Queen Jezebel.

It is important to understand that Israel was divided into two kingdoms. Think North and South during the Civil War in the United States of America. This division of Israel took place around 975 BC, right after the death of King Solomon. Solomon was the son of King David. When Solomon died, the kingdoms split into North (the Kingdom of Israel) and South (the Kingdom of Judah). Each kingdom obviously had a king.

Why did this happen? It had to do with a revolt against heavy taxation, but spiritually speaking, the kingdoms split because of the people's ongoing, deliberate disobedience to the commands of God.

So now we have a divided Israel for the next two hundred or so years. King Ahab and Queen Jezebel ruled the northern Kingdom of Israel for twenty-two years. The two of them were known for evil practices and the people feared them. Actually, it was Jezebel who persuaded her husband to worship false gods.

The main bulk of the story can be found in 1 Kings, which is found in the Old Testament of our Bibles. Let's jump in.

In 1 Kings 17, Elijah approached Ahab and said to him, "There isn't going to be rain unless I say so." That was bold considering all that King Ahab and his wife, Jezebel, were capable of. In the snap of a finger, they could have easily ordered Elijah to be killed on the spot. In fact, right after that statement, God was like, "Elijah, it's time for you to get out of Dodge, and I promise that I'll protect you."

Disclaimer here: unless it's specifically noted, I paraphrase a lot of the story and quotes. If I am quoting directly from the Bible, I'll most likely use the New Living Translation of the Bible throughout this book, unless otherwise stated. I'll say something like, "In such and such a book in such and such a chapter, this person says…"

So Elijah made this bold statement, and God was committed to protecting this prophet right away. As Elijah was sent into hiding, God even sent birds to deliver food to him. Think of this as an Uber Eats situation.

Shortly after Elijah got his nutrition, he met a widow, for whom he performed a miracle for her son because they were literally living paycheck to paycheck.

What was the miracle? Well, oil and flour were staple products during that time, and you needed them in order to practically live. Oil and flour were the main ingredients for most of the cooking. This poor widow was running out, which meant that she was in a desperate situation. Elijah came in and did what Jesus did while feeding the five thousand people in the New Testament. He miraculously multiplied the little that was there into an abundance!

It was not too long after this miracle took place when the widow's son died. After a brief exchange of words, Elijah performed the first biblical resurrection, and the little boy lived!

Okay, so all of that takes place in just one chapter! Elijah was off to a great start in ministry. Oh, who did I raise from the dead and what food did I multiply? Yeah, don't go there.

In the next chapter (18), God commanded Elijah to show himself to King Ahab. Mind you, King Ahab had posters everywhere that said "Most Wanted Man in the World." Not really, but Elijah was the most wanted man in the kingdom. Everyone was on the hunt for him. There were fugitive agents all over the place looking for Elijah so they could kill him. Remember, this was an agricultural society, so to prophesy no rain for 3.5 years meant you were basically pronouncing a death sentence on this society. Of course, the people wanted this prophet to be held accountable.

Ahab was a scary dude, and on his way to do as God commands, Elijah meets with Obadiah. Obadiah was a man of God who worked behind the scenes as an undercover agent for God in the government. Think of people who work in the government today and are Christians, even though they are not allowed to really be public with their faith.

When Jezebel ordered the prophets of God to be killed some time ago, Obadiah actually hid a hundred of them in two caves.

When Obadiah and Elijah meet, Elijah told Obadiah that the man King Ahab was looking for was ready to see him. Obadiah started to freak out and was sort of hesitant at first. Obadiah told Elijah that if he set up this meeting between Elijah and the king and Elijah got cold feet at the last minute and didn't show up, then it was Obadiah's head on the line. One can understand the hesitancy here.

After a brief encouragement from Elijah that he'd be there and that everything would be fine, Obadiah agreed. Now we saw King Ahab and Elijah meeting face to face.

When they meet, Elijah made a challenge to the king. Elijah, the troubler of Israel according to Ahab, challenged Ahab to a battle between the prophets of Baal and the true God of Israel.

Without getting into too much detail, Baal was a false god that the people of Israel worshiped a lot. In fact, Israel would often worship both the true God of Israel and the false gods around them. This is what keeps getting Israel in trouble in the first place! This is what warrants God judging them repeatedly.

Baal was a Canaanite-Phoenician god of fertility and weather, especially rainstorms. Without rain for all this time, the worship of Baal was very popular.

The moment comes and there's a gathering of 850 prophets of Baal and Asherah. These prophets were put in place by Jezebel, and they were strictly warned to only serve specific gods. If they didn't, then they would be killed. Jezebel placed prophets who would do and say what she desired. They've sold their souls to Jezebel, the one who hates the God of Israel.

Elijah basically says, "Have your prophets call upon your gods, and I'll call upon my God. We'll see who responds."

After agreeing, the prophets call on Baal but to no success. Baal does not respond.

In fact, while they are calling upon Baal and doing some crazy things like cutting themselves with knives and swords until the blood comes gushing out of them, Elijah mocks them all! "Where is your God? Has he not gotten up from his nap, or has he gone on vacation to Hawaii that he cannot respond?" Remember, my paraphrase, but he really does mock them!

When their efforts fail, Elijah prepares his space and calls upon God. It's Elijah's turn. It's showtime. When Elijah calls upon the Lord, fire from the Lord fell down from heaven and consumed the burnt offering that he prepared.

What an incredible moment! Can you imagine if that took place today with all those cell phones coming out of people's pockets to live stream for the whole world to see?

He then ordered all those prophets to be seized, and it tells us that Elijah slaughtered every single one of Baal's prophets.

While still in chapter 18, Elijah called on the rain to return after a 3.5-year drought. This was an intense storm brewing, and as Ahab got in his chariot to run away from the incoming storm, a supernatural strength came over Elijah, allowing him to outrun on foot the horses and chariots of King Ahab.

When all these dramatic events transpired, King Ahab went home and told his wife, Jezebel, everything that happened. Jezebel got super angry. After all, Elijah had just slaughtered all her own personal prophets. She was enraged.

Now in chapter 19, verse 2 tells us that Jezebel vowed to have Elijah killed within twenty-four hours. This was a serious commitment on her part. This was not bluffing.

Now we must take a moment to pause. These are two chapters, and this man of God has done so much in ministry. Actually, that's an understatement. I could only pray that I could do, in my entire lifetime, a small fraction of all that Elijah did up to this moment.

We can now speculate at the evilness of Jezebel. A man who had no problem slaughtering hundreds of prophets in public with his own bare hands was now intensely afraid of Jezebel's threat to have him found and killed within twenty-four hours. That should be enough to help you understand just how evil she really was.

Elijah was afraid, and he ran. In his fear, Elijah ran away into the forest, and it was there that he found a tree. He plopped his exhausted and weary body under this tree and prayed to God to take his life.

Whew.

Elijah was worn out, tired, exhausted, and just wanted to be home with the Lord. He didn't want to stay here any longer.

I am nowhere near where Elijah was at this point in his life, but there is a part of me that totally gets this idea of retreating, sitting under a tree, and sulking in despair. Elijah had every reason to feel this way, especially after reading all that we just read in two short chapters of the Bible. He had gone through a lot. He had been spiritually beaten up and was at the end of his rope.

Let me ask you a few questions: Are you under the tree feeling hopeless, tired, worn out, exhausted from the battles of life? Have you retreated from your normal patterns of life only to find yourself wondering what the purpose and meaning of life is right now?

Have you gone through seasons in life where you're like, "Lord, either come now or come take me to you"?

These are very real feelings, and I believe the Lord invites us to seek him in the midst of sitting under the tree. We come to sit under this tree for many reasons. Let's name them.

Maybe we've lost someone we love so much, and we just can't begin to think what it looks like to journey forward without that person anymore. Maybe we've been so emotionally, mentally, and spiritually abused as leaders in the church for so long that we're wondering where the reward is in serving in the church. Maybe we are having to witness someone we love so much go through the catastrophic effects of cancer or an illness that is taking a devastating toll on their bodies and minds.

Maybe we are in the midst of financial ruin, and we can't see any hope in the future. Maybe we're journeying through a nasty divorce, it just hurts so much, and we can't take another day of the pain. Maybe we were touched by a senseless tragedy, and the anger and pain is a feeling unlike anything we've ever experienced or felt before.

Maybe you feel so lonely and you feel that no one sees you anymore and you're just not certain that you have a purpose in life anymore. Maybe your mind is like this intense battle of emotions and it's completely shaking you to the core.

Maybe you feel that no one understands you, and they all think you're crazy, leaving you feeling in total despair. Maybe something you built up for many, many years comes tumbling down, and that's all you've ever known in life. Maybe you're in the middle of a court proceeding, and you feel so taken advantage of; or you feel that things have been distributed unfairly, that it's left you angry, bitter, and lonely. Maybe you're in the height of an intense addiction; you really, really want to get out of it, but no one wants to help except to condemn you. Maybe you are overcome by shame and guilt from something in the past, and it's eating you alive. Maybe you are tired of fighting for the right to be in the skin color you have, and you're sick of people looking at you like you're worth only a fraction of other people.

There is so much more we can add here, but all these things and more can send us into a season of depression, and this season can be either short-lived or extremely long. Some seasons feel like they'll never end. What we have here in 1 Kings 19 is a season of depression for Elijah, and he's had enough.

Now listen closely. It is not within my scope here to talk about what causes depression because it's a bit too complicated to simplify it. Because if we're being honest here, sometimes we get ourselves into the messes we're in, like the Israelites in the story of Gideon, and sometimes we're in the seasons of depression simply because we're broken people living in a broken world. Sometimes there's a direct cause, and sometimes it's just life.

However, the Lord is so kind and compassionate to meet us under the tree and minister to us like he did to Elijah, regardless of the cause.

In Exodus, another book in the Old Testament, we read, "The Lord, the Lord, a God merciful and gracious, slow to anger, and abounding in steadfast love and faithfulness, keeping steadfast love for thousands" (Exodus 34:6–7 ESV). Isn't that a beautiful picture of who God really is?

Take a look at what happens next in our story. An angel of the Lord touches Elijah, wakes him from his nap, and tells him to eat some cake and drink some water. What does Elijah do after he does as the angel of the Lord urges him to do? He goes back to nap again. I know that when I go through depression, I need to sleep. And sleep. And sleep. Elijah sleeps, gets up to eat, and then still isn't feeling it and heads back to sleep.

Then the angel of the Lord touches him again and urges Elijah to eat again. Right after that, God sends Elijah away for forty days and forty nights to Mount Sinai, where the Lord provides Elijah the strength he needs to make this journey. Not only does Elijah receive the strength he needs for the journey ahead, but Elijah got forty days and forty nights to walk alongside the Lord in solitude.

I'm going to stop there with our story of Elijah. There is more to his life, and I would encourage you to go back and keep reading.

I love this portion of Elijah's life from the time he sits under the tree through the time the Lord tends to him. I love it because it speaks to multiple layers we must be aware of when we're going through seasons of depression, sadness, and loneliness.

First, this story reminds us that we need to take care of ourselves by eating healthy and drinking lots of water. There is a physical aspect to being healed and maintaining strength that we must not neglect. As humans, we were designed to be fueled, and it's really important not to neglect this. But there is an important element of consuming a healthy diet as opposed to nonhealthy things that actually puts a toll on our body. It's all connected. When we eat badly, our body manifests that, and it begins to affect our mental and emotional state. We become what we take in.

Yes, I am perfectly aware that it was cake Elijah was fed! Hallelujah! This doesn't mean that transitioning to an all-cake diet is the answer! What it does mean, in my humble opinion, is that when I am sad, cake is within the parameters for me to digest! But in all seriousness, healthy eating is crucial. It may not always be the cause of why we feel the way we do, but things can get much worse if we neglect this important aspect of living.

Second, this story reminds us that we need to rest. You need to give your body and mind permission to rest and to be recharged. If you don't, life cannot and will not get better. Even Jesus took moments to get away to sleep.

We live in a society where we are constantly on the go. We live in a society where we think we can survive off very little sleep because there's so much to do. No, your body needs rest at a steady pace, and when we begin to experience our bodies and minds taking a hit, we need to rest; not push through. There is a sacredness to rest, and I think there is something for us to dwell on when Jesus tells us to take a Sabbath. You may think you're doing fine on very little sleep, but you're not. Just ask those closest to you. When I get exhausted and I try to push through, guess who is affected the most? My wife and kids.

Recently, I got sick. Like, really, really sick. It started just two days after hosting a major community event. I chalked it up to exhaustion and thought I would recover in a few days. I just needed a few days before the next big thing.

I was wrong. After a couple of weeks passed, I was not getting better. I was getting worse. I started to get exhausted, was unable to breathe well, and my chest would be in pain from time to time. After a series of doctor visits and a visit to the ER, I was found to have developed pneumonia. One doctor was absolutely certain that I had a combination of RSV and COVID that eventually translated to pneumonia. For forty-three days, I was depleted. Then I started to turn the corner. But even at that point, I knew that it would be a while before I could go full speed.

I knew that I needed to develop a habit of slowing down and resting more going forward. This was hard for me. I am a person who always wants to be on the go. To add to all this, the Christmas season was approaching, and this is a very busy time of the year for me as a pastor.

But God was more interested in teaching me the value of rest and instilling in me a slowness in my soul. There were other things He was teaching me, but that's for another book for another time.

Rest. You need rest. You need rest for your body and for your soul. The people around you need you to rest.

Third, this story reminds us that we need to retreat at times. We need vacations, personal days, and wellness days. We need to get away to clear our heads. We need to make sure that life isn't always about one single thing. We need to not work, work, work all the time. We need boundaries. We need moments where we can get out of the environment we've been in so long in order to see things differently or from a different perspective. Sometimes seeing from the outside gives us a new understanding than trying to see from the inside.

For me, I like to retreat to the ocean because it's where I feel the most calm; where I can "hear" from Jesus. It's where my spirit gets settled. It's where I can find the space to pause the noise of life. I need retreat times. If I don't take retreat times, I find that I start to become the version of myself that I hate.

Now you may be thinking that you can't afford to retreat due to cost and time. I totally get that, but hear this: you can't afford not to.

Allow me to define a retreat. It doesn't always mean an overnight or an extended time away. But for your wife, it may mean giving her a night away at a hotel for her to breathe. It may mean taking an afternoon once a month to find your perfect spot and to sit in it. Retreating is getting away from the "normal" from time to time so you don't end up depleted. Listen, there is nothing heroic about pushing through the demands of life and proving that you did it. No, what's heroic is retreating so that the people who love you get the best version of you.

For Elijah, the Lord took him away for forty days and forty nights. The Lord was basically saying to Elijah, "I'm taking you away from ministry for a short while so I can replenish your soul." It is to that we turn next.

Fourth, the story here reminds us that we need to be tended to by the Lord. If the mighty prophet of God needed to be tended to by the Lord, then you do too. You need the touch of the Lord, and sometimes it means Him touching you in places of your life where you've rejected past healing from. Sometimes we've allowed the Lord to touch certain areas and not others, and it's caught up to us. Sometimes we've poured so much into the lives of others that we forget that we need to be poured into too. At some point, you'll be empty. The only way to be filled again is by the Lord, and nothing or no one else can do that for you.

For me, being touched by the Lord means finding quiet times to intentionally hear from the Lord. It means not using my sermon preparation time as my devotion time. It doesn't work. It means journaling. It means putting on worship songs. It means reading the Bible to hear from the Lord; not just about the Lord. It means being still and knowing that the Lord is good and gracious and merciful. It means getting to the point in our lives where we say, "Lord, I only have myself to offer, and I'm giving it to you." When we only have that small glowing ember, it's a good time to intentionally be replenished by God.

This one is important because we will try to be touched by other things outside of the Lord, and we will receive the illusion that we're ready to move on when we're not. God desires to heal you if you'll let Him. Jesus constantly is asking us, "Do you want to get well?"

I may not have found myself under a literal tree, but I found myself alone at the fire pit, and the point is that we're often brought to a point that screams, "You can't keep going on like this." If we can soften our facade a bit, let's admit that nothing else is working, isn't it? So many people are trying to plod through life without Christ, and it's absolutely miserable.

No one is exempt from finding themselves under "the tree." It doesn't matter if you're a so-called godly leader or if you're not. We're all human, and it's a grave mistake to take the humanness out of the biblical characters. They have something to teach us here about what it means to be human. It is okay to cry, to scream, to question, to yell out, to be angry, to be emotional, to feel weak. When we try to stuff all this down, it doesn't go away.

Imagine if you could put a cover on top of a volcano that's just begun to erupt. Suppose that you are successful in putting on the lid. Eventually, the lava is going to come out elsewhere at another time. It's the same way with untended wounds. You may have thought that you've handled a past memory until it comes creeping up twenty years later. You may think you have dealt with the past until it comes back into your later years of marriage and parenthood. And the kindness of God is that he doesn't want you to put a lid on it. He wants to heal you. He wants to meet you where you are. He wants to sit under the tree with you. He won't leave you there though. That doesn't mean this gives license for Christians to put a time limit on your healing process. It doesn't mean it gives us license to do that to others.

So often, we want fast results. We want overnight success. But what is success on the Christian journey? Is it that we've somehow arrived somewhere? Or is it that we've allowed ourselves to meet God in the midst of life and be touched by Him? And where are we going so fast? Why are we in such a rush? I think we need to slow down just a bit. We need to understand that God is not only the sanctification God of A (birth) to Z (death) but is also the sanctification God of AB and C (all of life). He is a God of the process. Life does matter.

Sanctification is just a fancy word that describes the life-long journey God takes us all on to mold us into the person He desires us to be.

It's just that so often we highlight that moment we've surrendered to Jesus and sort of not think about what comes next. All eyes are on the day He comes back and when we "get to heaven." We think that the morning after we've surrendered to Jesus, we're going to be 100 percent perfect, never struggle again, and 100 percent be healed in 100 percent of all areas of our lives. It's like putting all our chips into the wedding and not investing much in the marriage.

So here we are with just a small glowing ember in our possession. In holding this ember, we feel we've got nothing much to offer; that we've somehow failed because we've supposedly succumbed to a weakness in our emotions. Yet while we're hoping for this ember to ignite a raging flame of exterior success, the Lord wants to place this ember in your soul and reignite a raging flame of interior revival and healing.

What does it profit you to look good on the outside and do all these amazing things in life and ministry and for all to see yet have your soul crumbling to pieces?

The story of Elijah has a lot to teach us.

When we come to the tree like Elijah did, we learn that God can take your shattered pieces and make something beautiful.

I once heard about a Japanese art technique where shattered pieces of pottery are repaired by mending the areas of breakage with lacquer and gold. It's a process known as *kintsugi*. When the process is finished, the pottery is put together, and one can see that the pottery used to be in pieces. Yet the finished product truly is beautiful.

When I think about this process, I think that God does something similar to us when we feel we're in a thousand pieces. He mends us by touching us and the gold that mends us together is His grace, His kindness, His compassion, His understanding, and His love for you.

So, friend, if you're under the tree, then you're in a good spot if you'll let Jesus touch you.

The love that Jesus has for you is so indescribable. Take a look at a Bible passage that I really want you to grasp. It's from a letter to an ancient church, called Ephesus. The letter is Ephesians and is written by a man named Paul. It's found in the New Testament portion of the Bible.

In it, Paul writes, "And may you have the power to understand, as all God's people should, how wide, how long, how high, and how deep His love is" (Ephesians 3:17).

What Paul is saying is this: God's love for you, despite all your flaws and imperfections and unstable emotions, has no suitable vocabulary to describe it accurately. In fact, you'll need supernatural help from God to even begin to understand the measurement of His love for you. Isn't that crazy!

So friend, allow His love to touch you; to tend to your soul.

CHAPTER 2

Heman the Ezrahite (Dark Night of the Soul)

One of the things I love about the Psalms in the Bible—and there are 150 of them, by the way—is that they are just so real, raw, unfiltered, and honest. They deal with real circumstances, real emotions, real situations, and they just lay it out as it is.

Of course, there are Psalms that highlight the highs of life, and we certainly do love singing those Psalms in church and, if you're in a traditional setting, turning them into responsive readings.

Years ago, I served as an associate pastor at a small Baptist church in New England and one of my jobs was to select the Psalm for the upcoming Sunday. My job was to take this Psalm and turn it into a responsorial reading (where I read a verse, the congregation read a verse, and so on until the Psalm was completed).

I remember flipping through Psalms, and I came across a particular one that piqued my interest for some reason. At first, I was like, *My goodness, what am I reading?* I read it through over and over again and decided it would be the Psalm of choice for that upcoming Sunday.

When one of the elders caught wind of my selection (because it had to be approved beforehand), it was immediately turned down.

"People don't want to hear about that kind of stuff," he said. He went on to say, "Sundays are supposed to be happy and filled with such joy."

Yeah, I get that (I think?), but on any given Sunday, there are people coming who are not feeling a ton of joy and need to be reminded that they have permission to be in the valley sometimes and be reminded that Christ meets them in the valley. I think one of the biggest missed targets in today's church is walking alongside people who are venturing through the valley and discipling them on what it means to follow Christ in the valley. So often, we're taught to avoid and escape suffering and dark valleys at all costs. This is very true in the West. But life isn't always roses and sunshine and we need to disciple our people on what it means to cling onto hope in such circumstances.

One of the greatest victories we claim as Christians is that the valley experiences don't have the final say. At the same time, we must not chide people in saying, "Listen, get a grip on life, have more faith in the victory of the end times, and turn that frown upside down." I mean, we probably wouldn't necessarily say that, but we sure are good at distancing ourselves from those going through seasons of pain, because it's somehow uncomfortable for us.

The writer of Ecclesiastes, who is Solomon by the way, writes this to us: "For everything there is a season, a time for every activity under heaven… A time to cry and a time to laugh. A time to grieve and a time to dance" (3:1,4). While holding this truth in one hand, there is another truth in the other hand, and it goes like this: "Be happy with those who are happy, and weep with those who weep" (Romans 12:15).

So the challenge here for us is to create spaces for people to go through seasons and to enter into those spaces with them. Journey with them. The encouragement here is that the Bible absolutely gives you permission to feel the way that you do but also provides a glimpse into the light at the end of the tunnel. I believe that God does something quite beautiful in the midst of our dark seasons. It may not seem like it, but when I look back at those seasons, I am thankful because those seasons prepared me for things to come in life.

I'll admit a word of caution here: some people are going through unimaginable pain in life, and the last thing you want to say to that person is, "God must be preparing you for something greater to come." I do not believe God purposefully inflicts all bad things on a person for the sole purpose of preparing them for what's ahead. But I do believe that, through the power and comfort of the Holy Spirit, we can choose to rise out of the ashes and let our experiences create something truly beautiful ahead.

It took me a long time of questioning my past experiences before I could see the good that came out of them. This does not mean that the experiences I went through were good. It means that I've allowed God to use my past experiences to be a blessing to others. For example, I went through terrible things as a child in the foster care system. The good that came from it, or the blessing for others that came from it? Adopting two beautiful kids today and adding them to my family. Being more compassionate today to those kids who are in the system. Inspiring others to hop on board the mission to adopt in the same way that Joseph adopted baby Jesus.

Actually, the more I think about the blessings and the good that came from my negative experiences in the system, the more I realize just how long that list really is.

Before we turn our attention to the Psalm that I was forbidden to turn into a responsive reading in 2014, let me share with you a personal story of a time that I felt somewhat similar to the writer of this Psalm.

I am not sure exactly what year it was; I was a middle schooler, and I was going through a lot in life. I was living with my grandparents at the time, and I remember that my grandmother and I got into a heated argument. That took place quite often, actually. I don't even remember what the argument was about; I do remember my reaction, and I do remember the things that were stirring in my heart. I remember the intensity in my heart and the anger that took over my body.

I screamed, ran out the door, and slammed the door behind me to further reinforce my true feelings. It was night. It was dark outside, and there was an intense storm raging. It was raining like crazy, and I didn't even have shoes on.

For whatever reason, my mother was at the house that night. I never lived with my mother except for the first year or so of my life. I'll tap more into that at a later time.

The rain was torrential, and the thunder was loud. I ran down the street as my mother and my grandmother yelled at me to come back. I didn't listen. I was not going to go back. I'd had enough. I kept running and running, and when I noticed that my mother's car was coming down the street just moments later, I quickly found the nearest bush and basically plunged myself into it so I could hide. I stayed in that bush for nearly an hour (at least it seemed that way), and it seemed like the search party for me eventually ended.

I didn't have a plan. I was a minor. What was I going to do? A thought occurred to me that I could go another three miles or so to my great-grandfather's house and seek refuge there. Of course, they would be looking for me there at some point. I contemplated my plan, and before I executed it, I wept. I broke down. I broke down so much that I couldn't even produce any more tears but could feel my soul in such anguish. I was desperate. You ever cry out and no noise comes out? Yeah, that's what it felt like. I truly hated life and wanted nothing to do with anyone in it. I didn't want to live.

Why was I so angry? What was going on? I was at a point in my life where all those foster care years caught up to me, as well as the experiences I was going through. I was not in a good place. Middle school sucked, and I constantly got bullied, always got into fights, spent countless days in detention, spent numerous occasions in in-house suspension, and was suspended twice for a month or more each time. I wasn't a good kid, but what I wish could have happened at that moment was for someone to see me, to hear me. I wanted someone to understand me and to truly know what all those former years in the foster care system were really like.

I was acting out in life because I had so much pain built up inside of me. I was also behaving in a certain way because I was developing a survivalist mentality. There's been so much hurt in my life, and I just knew that the only one who could protect me, or wanted to, anyway, was myself.

I was given up by my mother at such a little age and then thrown into the foster care system. My mother struggled with drugs growing up. My father left before I was even born. When I entered into the foster care system, I got passed between multiple homes for years. Of course, memory can be blurred but what can't be blurred is the trauma. That sticks with you forever. You may not remember exact names or the color of the houses you lived in, but you remember the screaming, the kicking, the beatings, the abuse; and all of that eclipses any good memories (not that there were any). No, for real, there really weren't any good memories.

Some homes were better than others, but to be honest, they were all terrible as far as I can remember. Even the "best" home housed the sexual abuser who stole my dignity at age five or six. One home housed a foster father who came home drunk frequently and would kick me in the stomach, smash a beer bottle over my neck and back, and throw me around until he passed out drunk on the couch.

In the "best" home (and I say "best" because the foster mom and father were good people), there was a foster brother who sexually molested me just about every day for a good part of my time there. I couldn't get away, couldn't cry out because he would threaten me. What was I supposed to do with the person who was in charge of babysitting me often? And how was I supposed to process what was happening to me at five years old?

Five-year-olds are supposed to be throwing the ball around with their dads, rollerblading at the rink, coloring, watching *Scooby-Doo*, rolling down grassy hills, laughing, jumping around, wrestling with dad, and eating ice cream. And maybe I did some of these things like coloring, but when you are over-powered by an adult who does whatever he pleases with you, does any of that even matter anymore?

Well, anyway, the foster care era eventually came to an end, and I ended up with my grandparents, but I carried with me an intense amount of pain and anger. It all started off with a year of silence where I wouldn't speak to anyone.

I did go to a number of therapists, and people have tried to "fix" me, but none of them knew what happened in foster care. I never told anyone except a few people once I got into my later years of high school. That is a heavy secret to carry. I felt ashamed. I felt I deserved it. I felt lonely. I felt insecure. I felt abandoned. And what's crazy is that the effects of all that never truly go away completely.

To this day, I still struggle with trust. Sometimes I withhold it completely, and sometimes I give it out freely in the hope of being convinced that maybe there are still people who can be trusted.

I struggle to decompress, and sometimes I struggle with coping. Now I've come a long way since many years ago, but I still have to work hard at things. When I get upset, I need to take some time alone to decompress. When I am sad or frustrated, I need to talk things out with a person I love before I can move on to the next thing. When I struggle to communicate, I need to write it out as a way of processing what's inside. When I feel insecure, which is often, I need to be reminded that everything will be okay.

It's just the way it is sometimes, but I am thankful that God has brought me this far and has put people in my life like Victoria, my bride, to be extra understanding and patient.

So here I am at my grandparents', and after the year of silence, I started to act out. I began with behavior patterns that I couldn't quite understand myself. I went into survival mode. And then it grew to turning to the streets. I got into a lot of trouble and was constantly running into the police. I fought a lot, and sometimes it would get out of control as this rage bubbled inside of me. I drank a lot in elementary school, shoplifted, and did anything I could to prove I was cool to my friends. But deep inside, I was hurting.

All kinds of questions were stirring in my mind. My grandparents took me to church often, and I decided to live a double life. I would model the good Christian boy while at church and at church events, but I absolutely hated church, Christians, and wondered how a good, all-powerful God could allow a little boy to be so defenseless against extremely abusive people. What I shared above doesn't even begin to scratch the surface of all the things that I went through.

Where was God then? Where was God now? Did He hear me? Did He care about me? Did He want anything to do with a broken vessel like me?

I do realize that despite my upbringing being so traumatic, many people have gone through this and are currently going through this. I don't pretend that my story is somehow "worse" than yours or many others. Your story matters, and it doesn't matter which story is more traumatic because pain is pain and trauma is trauma, no matter the shape and form of it.

That night, as I hid in those bushes, I cried out to God all those questions I had for him. I wanted to die. I wanted to end my life because there was absolutely no way a good future was in store. I decided to head to my great grandfather's home because I knew he was a gun collector, and I knew that he would open the doors for me to come in. My body started to shake, I started to vomit, I started to tremble, and I started the trek. That was a long three-mile journey.

I arrived at his home, and as expected, he was there waiting for me. He took me in and allowed me to shower, fed me, and then sat me down. He didn't give me a talk. He listened to me. In a sense, he talked me off the "edge," but I was not so sure of what was ahead for me. I was in a complete mess, and I had feelings inside me that I couldn't describe. On top of all this, my relationship with my grandmother was extremely rocky. Of course, I gave them a run for their money, but if only they knew the experiences and memories I carried. Maybe then they could come to resolutions that it wasn't my fault that I was who I was. Not entirely, anyway. No little child should ever have to experience certain things.

Unfortunately, this happens every single day to varying degrees across America, and I will always be an advocate for good foster parents. The problem is that there are too many foster parents who give up on the kids when they behave in a way that isn't necessarily their fault. We get passed around from house to house, and eventually, we just never stick anymore. You ever rip a piece of duct tape and put it on a surface? It sticks the first time, and then it loses its stickiness the more you rip it up and put it back on. Some foster parents take in kids to do to them what was done to them.

That's a topic for another time. I just wanted to give you some context to what led me to feel the way I did that night. I did eventually go back "home," but the next few years were intense.

Alright. So that Psalm I was forbidden to "expose" to the church? It's Psalm 88, and I want to share it with you.

But let me start off by saying this: this is an intense Psalm. I want you to know that reading it may be difficult for you, depending on your experiences, but please know that there is so much hope I'm going to follow up on. Believe me, I was at a point in my life where I never went beyond this Psalm and just accepted defeat and despair. While all our experiences are different from each other, please know that I validate your experiences and the Lord really, really, does care. This Psalm is an inspired Word of God. Let's begin.

Heman, the author of this Psalm, was a grandson of Samuel, who was the final judge of Israel in the Bible who anointed King Saul and King David, Israel's first two kings (yes, I know, God was Israel's first King). In 1 Chronicles 25:5, we learn that God gave Heman fourteen sons and three daughters. Just an average-size family. His name means "faithful," and he was appointed by King David as one of the leaders of the temple music program. Psalm 88 is the only Psalm of the 150 we have that's attributed to his authorship.

Psalm 88 begins this way:

> O Lord, God of my salvation, I cry out to
> you by day. I come out to you at night. Now hear
> my prayer, listen to my cry. (verses 1–2)

Notice that Heman's depression doesn't take him away from God; it throws him toward God. And he's asking God to please hear him. He is in anguish both day and night. For this guy, joy did not come in the morning.

Perhaps you've felt that way. Even at night, you soak your pillows with your tears, and the sorrow just doesn't seem to go away. Heman is approaching God and basically is saying, "I'm bringing to you my sorrow, and I just hope you'll see me, hear me, listen to me."

The next portion of Psalm 88 goes like this:

> For my life is full of troubles, and death draws near. I am as good as dead, like a strong man with no strength left. They have left me among the dead, and I lie like a corpse in a grave. I am forgotten, cut off from your care. (verses 3–5)

I told you it was pretty dark. This is total desperation, and I think the church has a lot to learn about how we pray. So often, we pray in an orderly fashion, but Heman prays with honesty, messiness, and boldness. And God isn't turning Heman away.

I remember being in a prayer circle some years ago, and it was somewhat orderly. We would take turns praying and just go in a circle. Each person prayed a specific prayer, and they sort of all sounded the same.

And then this woman begins to pray, and she prayed in a way I've never heard. It was the type of prayer that gave off the impression she was going through some difficult things in her life. But she clung onto God and didn't let go. She was brutally honest, exceptionally bold, and was very emotional. She cried loudly, and while some found the situation a bit uncomfortable, I was mesmerized by her approach.

Her prayer approach reminded me of this parable that Jesus gives in the Gospel of Luke.

In this parable (Luke 18), there was a judge who had absolutely no fear of God, and he didn't care about the people he presided over.

A widow would approach the judge and demand that justice be delivered in her dispute with an enemy of hers.

The judge ignored her and pushed her off to the side. Then, after this widow keeps nagging the judge with her request, this judge, who doesn't typically care for the people or fear God, ends up giving this widow the justice she wants. This widow was wearing down the judge with her constant requests.

Jesus tells his disciples this parable as a way of telling them that they should always pray and never give up. Be persistent in our approach to God.

The woman in that prayer circle came back and prayed in that intense way for weeks upon weeks. She was persistent and she was living some sort of valley experience that forced her to be desperate. There is something about prayers out of desperation that's powerful.

In many of our churches, we tend to avoid people like her, or we red-list her as someone who needs extreme psychiatric care. No, people like her really believe that God is real and will go to any length to cling onto this God until He answers.

Heman goes on to pray, "You have thrown me into the lowest pit, into the darkest depths. Your anger weighs me down; with wave after wave you have engulfed me" (verses 6–7).

Heman isn't getting bitter here. He is articulating to God that what he knows about God in his head isn't matching what he's experiencing. You ever feel that way? You know what the Bible says about the goodness, mercy, grace, and splendor of God, but you aren't really feeling loved by Him right now. You feel distant. You feel cut off from the favor of God. You feel He's abandoned you. You see God "coming through" for other people, yet what about you?

Now we don't exactly know what verses 6–7 are talking about because it does seem that Heman is in the situation he's in right now because of something he did. This is evidenced by the phrase "your anger weighs me down." We're not told any details. Why is this? Because it doesn't matter. Because God still invites us to bring our emotions to Him, and He is so willing to "touch us" and to heal us regardless of cause.

This is a Psalm that can be cried out from a prison cell or from the empty room of a child you lost unexpectedly. Why is that? Because God's grace and kindness knows no bounds.

This next section of Psalm 88 unfolds this way:

> You have driven my friends away by making me repulsive to them. I am in a trap with no way of escape. My eyes are blinded by my tears. Each day I beg for your help, O Lord; I lift my hands to you for mercy. Are your wonderful deeds of

> any use to the dead? Do the dead rise up and praise you? (verses 8–10)

Heman wants to have God shower him with compassion, and Heman wants to be able to praise God as a result of it. He wants God to "come through" for him so he can praise Him for it. What he's really saying is, "If I am dead, then it can't happen." There is an urgency in Heman's prayer. He is crying out to God to not let him die like this. He is persistent. He won't let go until God answers, and this is the type of prayer we are to pray when we're in anguish. Cling to the anchor of hope we have in Jesus.

Heman goes on to say, "Can those in the grave declare your unfailing love? Can they proclaim your faithfulness in the place of destruction? Can the darkness speak of your wonderful deeds? Can anyone in the land of forgetfulness talk about your righteousness? O Lord, I cry out to you. I will keep on pleading day by day. O Lord, why do you reject me? Why do you turn your face from me?" (verses 11–14).

One of the great benefits you and I have today that was really only foreshadowed in the Old Testament is the knowledge of what Jesus has done once and for all. The whole Old Testament is a promise that someone will be sent to ultimately rescue them from the helpless situation they find themselves in. Heman could only hope and have faith in the promise of a redeemer, but it is we today that already know that this Promised One has come and disarmed the powers and authorities. His name is Jesus.

Heman was wondering if there really was any hope once he died. He was in a dark place because now he felt that God had turned his face on him, and he imagined that he would die like this, and that was it. The beauty for us today is that death isn't the final destination, and death does not have the final say because Jesus came and said "Checkmate" to the devil when He resurrected from the dead. Heman was living in an advent period waiting for the Promised One. We are living in an advent period waiting for the resurrected Jesus to come riding on a horse and make all things new.

Let's see what else is in store as we turn to the end of Psalm 88:

> I have been sick and close to death since my youth. I stand helpless and desperate before your terrors. Your fierce anger has overwhelmed me. Your terrors have paralyzed me. They swirl around me like floodwaters all day long. They have engulfed me completely. You have taken away my companions and loved ones. Darkness is my closest friend.

Whew. My goodness. What an ending here. Your best friend is darkness.

You know, as I reflect on this Psalm, I see a man with tremendous faith despite the darkness that envelops him. If he didn't have faith, he wouldn't keep coming back to God crying out. He still has a small glowing ember and hasn't given up on God; and this is so important for you to hear. We may think that it is all doom and gloom here and wonder what's the purpose in this Psalm, but this Psalm is all about trusting in and having faith in God when we "feel" like he's absent.

This can be a really foreign concept in many of today's churches, for our preaching and church culture tend to be centered on our happiness. This Psalm is brutal. It's honest. It's dark. It isn't this amazing, alluring theological present with a giant bow on it. This Psalm reminds us that being redeemed by Jesus doesn't mean we get a hall pass on life's brutal realities. If we think we deserve this hall pass, we might want to reassess whether we're more in love with the gifts of God or the giver of those gifts, God himself.

For Heman, apparently, he's been feeling this miserable for basically his entire life. That's rough.

So it is complete nonsense when someone attributes our depression, loneliness, and sadness to a lack of faith. It is completely possible to know God "as the God of [your] salvation" and feel like He isn't going to come through for you today. It is completely possible to hold in tension belief and doubt. It is completely possible to know what the Bible says about the kindness of God and feel that His kindness has gone away.

As I keep thinking about the Psalm, one thing that comes to mind immediately is the fact that these are emotions that every single human being is capable of feeling regardless of age, sex, religion, and location. It's universal. And as I reflect even more on this, I am at a loss on how someone can go through dark seasons without any belief anchored anywhere. This isn't an attack on people who claim no belief in God; it's wondering what gets you through difficult seasons if life truly is living and then dying and nothing else.

If you think about it, when it comes to suffering, depression, and anguish, what's the response of all worldviews, philosophies, and religions? I do know that Christianity stands out as unique. It stands out because God loved us so much that he came down to rescue you. In doing so, he "himself has gone through suffering and testing" (Hebrews 2:18). He didn't stay in heaven. He took upon our pain. He knows what we go through. He relates.

People ask, "What is Christianity's answer to the suffering that's universal?" I always say, "Jesus and what He did."

When Jesus was nailed to the cross, "at about three o'clock, [He] called out with a loud voice, 'Eli, Eli, lema sabachthani!' which means, 'My God, My God, why have you abandoned me?'" (Matthew 27:46).

Two things we can take from that statement: the first is that Jesus knows what it's like to be in the valley with you. The second is that Jesus experienced abandonment on the cross so that you never will be forsaken. We may feel that He's abandoned us, but He hasn't. He is right there with you. We may feel that our valley experiences are never going to end, but they will.

When I look at the story of Jesus, I see a God who completely understands the pain and suffering we experience. It grieves Him. Jesus had very real emotions. In fact, we see that before Jesus was to be handed over to the authorities, Jesus "prayed more fervently, and he was in such agony of spirit that his sweat fell to the ground like great drops of blood" (Luke 22:44).

And I know that life can be so darn difficult at times, and it seems like it's an eternity of suffering. But let me encourage you here in quoting the Apostle Paul: "For our present troubles are small and won't last very long. Yet they produce for us a glory that vastly outweighs them and will last forever! So we don't look at the troubles we can see now; rather, we fix our gaze on things that cannot be seen. For the things we see now will soon be gone, but the things we cannot see will last forever" (2 Corinthians 4:17–18).

I like this passage, and I cling to it in seasons of depression and sadness because all of those things will one day be no more. The people we've lost we will see in heaven. The injustices we've experienced will be made right. The tears we shed will be no more. The pain we endure will go away. Does any of this make life easy right now? No, it doesn't. But Jesus gives us something here to cling to that no other worldview or religion offers.

I shared Psalm 88 because it tells us we can run to God in the midst of our struggles. We can still be faithful followers of Jesus and still cry out, shout, question, wrestle, be sad, be lonely, and be struggling with belief. We can run into the arms of God with just a small glowing ember. We can run to God and be completely honest and open with him.

Sometimes we feel that God is done with us, that God wants nothing more to do with us, that God is annoyed by us, that God is turned off by us. But that's not true. God is the Creator of the universe and the heavens and can handle what we bring Him. After all, He already knows. He already knew. He just doesn't desire that we go through the valley alone.

Allow me to wrap up this section by sharing with you the story of William Cowper, who was a famous hymn writer that lived from 1731 to 1800 and wrote a couple of famous hymns such as "God Moves in a Mysterious Way" and "There Is a Fountain Filled with Blood."

I know there seems to be a movement away from the world of hymns, but I personally am a fan of them because of the rich history, theology, and rootedness that's in them. I think there is tremendous value in spending some time with the hymns. Don't get me wrong here. I do love some of our modern songs of praise, but there's something about hymns that anchors my soul to the depths of who God is.

For the last decade or so, I've always taken the hymns we would sing at various churches I served at and looked up the "story" behind them. This allowed me to sing with a whole other level of commitment. For example, we're all most likely familiar with the famous hymn "It Is Well with My Soul." If you're not, stop right there and look it up. The band, Kutless, has a pretty awesome rendition of it.

The words are rich. Yet they become richer when you find out that Horatio Spafford, the author of the hymn, wrote the words over the spot in the ocean where his four daughters tragically lost their lives when the *Ville du Havre* sank to the bottom of the ocean. It was the worst disaster in naval history until the sinking of the *Titanic* forty years later.

Horatio could pen the words "It is well with my soul" despite the tragedy he endured. Every time I sing the hymn, I am strengthened.

So who is William Cowper and what does he have to do with depression and what we're talking about? Everything.

When Cowper was five years old, his mother died. When he was in school, he was treated terribly by a bully, and it led to Cowper's depression. As he got older, he went to law school, which ended up being a total failure because he was deathly afraid of the oral examinations. He brought himself to a state of madness around that time and attempted suicide, which landed him in an asylum. When he was in the asylum, he read a verse from the book of Romans (found in the New Testament of the Bible), and he said he immediately became converted. This book was left for Cowper by the attending doctor at the asylum who loved Jesus.

Shortly after this, he moved to Olney, where he met John Newton, the pastor who wrote "Amazing Grace." John Newton became Cowper's pastor and quickly grew concerned about Cowper's depression. To help Cowper stay on track, John Newton decided to invite Cowper to coauthor a book of hymns, called the *Olney Hymns*. Cowper ended up authoring sixty-eight of those hymns, some of which are now a part of the hymnal of many traditional churches.

During the period of writing these Olney Hymns, Cowper's brother died, and it took a long time for Cowper to mentally recover from this. As he neared death in 1800, Cowper still struggled with severe depression. He went into a severe season of depression four times and attempted suicide three times. When he died, he did not die cheerfully. He was in a state of despair.

This is just a glimpse into the life of William Cowper. Here was a man who deeply loved Jesus and wrote some of the most majestic pieces of poetry known to mankind. After all, he was mentored by the great, renowned John Newton. Here was a man who revered Jesus, yet he experienced a level of depression similar to Heman, the author of Psalm 88.

Is William Cowper in the full presence of Jesus right now? Absolutely! I think that one of the things we forget about the Christian journey is that God is at work in us, through the Spirit, each and every single day. The process of the Christian journey is exactly that—a process. While some things may do a complete turn-around the day we surrender to Jesus, most things don't. Oftentimes, we are working on a number of things in our lives for many, many years. None of us will spiritually "arrive" this side of eternity. But we long to be on the other side, and that's the hope we can cling to.

I know, this was probably a tough chapter to read through. It drained me writing it, but I am hoping that you were able to see that struggling with depression, with sadness, and with loneliness does not mean you lack faith, does not mean you're a second-class Christian citizen, does not mean that God is repelled by you, and it does not mean that it's somehow hindering a great potential that God wants to do in you. No, we need to begin to see that God is at work in the midst of all seasons.

Let me encourage you in saying this: no matter how dark some of our seasons can get, there is still an ember that's glowing. Want to know how I know that? Because God woke you up this morning and has given you a new day. Sure, maybe it was so difficult to pull yourself out of bed, but you did. I'm proud of you. Don't be afraid to take that tiny, small glowing ember and keep bringing it to God and ask Him loudly to do a miracle. Be persistent. Be loud. Be bold.

For the church, create spaces for people to venture through the valley. Oftentimes, we want quick fixes. Sometimes God does a quick fix, and sometimes He doesn't. Just remember that the people going through valley experiences don't want to be in those valleys any more than you want them to get out of it.

Create spaces of healing. Create a culture of patience. Listen, I am going to get really honest here: a church culture that's all about that one-hour on Sunday morning is going to push people in the valley away. Walking with people in all stages of life is going to take more than just one hour a week. We need to recover a theology of what it means to do life together as Christian brothers and sisters; to check in on one another Monday through Saturday and to enter difficult spaces with a beam of hope.

CHAPTER 3

Job
(Integrity)

When I was reflecting on which Bible character to work with here, Job immediately came to mind. I mean, the dude lost just about everything! For him, when it rained, it poured. The storms were torrential. I'm not exaggerating here either. You'll see, but for now, here's the inspiration for me when I look at his life: despite going through astronomical seasons of loss, Job never cursed God.

Was he perfect and sinless? Of course not. Who is? Did he have times when he was irritable, upset, angry, frustrated, and annoyed? Yup.

But Job strived to remain a man of integrity. He strived to follow the Lord when it was *tough to do so*. Did he have seasons when he doubted whether or not he should follow God? Of course! But take a look at what he says: "Though he slay me, I will hope in him" (Job 13:15).

"Though he slay me, I will hope in him." Just let the implications of that reverberate throughout your soul. Sit with it for a moment.

"Though God brings me through the fire of life, I will praise him. Though God gives and takes away, I will praise him. Though God shuts a door I've worked so hard to open and go through, I will praise him. Though God shatters my dreams, I will praise him."

Go ahead. Fill in the blank. "Though God _____ I will praise him. I will put my hope in him."

Let's lay all our cards on the table. If we're completely honest, we're all going to be tested in a way that asks us if God is enough for us when all else is taken away. Do we, in our struggles, run to God, or do we run away from God?

I know that for me, it's easy to complain, become so bitter, and to put on a self-pity show when something doesn't go my way in life. I'll confess something to you. I'm a little weak in this area. Okay, very weak! I'll give my list to God of all that went wrong on any given day, and then He'll give me a list back of his blessings that's a trillion times longer.

The other day, it seemed like nothing was going right. You ever have one of those days? You lose your keys on a very important workday. After finally finding those keys, you get a flat tire on the way to work. After getting the tire fixed, you spill your entire cup of coffee on your dress shirt and pants. After running to the store to get a new outfit, you realize you forgot your money at home. And on and on it goes.

But then God reminds me that I have healthy kids, a roof over my head, a beautiful and charming wife, a full-time job, a steady income, a computer to type these words… And most importantly, I have Him who laid His life down for me. That's a sobering reality when you let that thought soak in you.

But we don't always think this way as a default, do we? And it's incredibly hard to think this way when we're really in the trenches.

When I've gone through seasons of depression, when there's only a small ember left, I've questioned whether or not I should remain in ministry. I thought, *There are so many other things I could be doing right now that'll be more fun, allow me to have more time at home, and bring in more money for my family.* I thought, *Why am I putting up with some of the things I put up with when I can easily just walk away and do something else?* I've also thought at times, "It's just easier to walk away from the faith and do all the things I see everyone else doing that appear to be bringing them joy."

Pause right there. Imagine for a moment if God gave up on us? Imagine if Jesus, after all that he was going through in the gospels, just said, "You know what? These people don't deserve all the misery I'm about to endure for them. I'm done."

Jesus had every opportunity to give up on us, but he didn't. In Luke 9:51, it says, "As the time drew near for him to ascend to heaven, Jesus resolutely set out for Jerusalem." Jerusalem is where he would lay his life down for us, willingly. The eyes of Jesus set on Jerusalem was a common theme in the gospels. Why is this? Because Jesus came for the sole purpose and mission of redeeming you, despite how difficult it would all be; despite how much we would fail him over and over again. He resolved to do this no matter what.

And when I begin to think that the grass is greener on the other side of giving up the call that God put on my life, I'm being deceived, and the enemy knows it. Shortly, when we take a more in-depth look at the life of Job, we'll see that Job could have easily thrown his hands up in the air and said, "I'm done." This man has lost so much. His friends even tried to find the source of his suffering by laying blame in areas that were completely off base. The enemy would love nothing more than for you to wring your hands, throw in the towel, and pursue your own course of action.

When we go through those dark seasons, the enemy starts to creep in and make promises. He'll say, "Listen, just walk away from God, and I'll provide something entirely better." He'll bring you the contract of all the things that would be pleasing to your eye and say, "It's all yours if you'll just sign your name right there."

"Just curse God. Just walk away. Just pursue what your heart desires."

He did this with Jesus. Jesus was out in the wilderness one day, and the devil tempted Jesus with a series of things. We can find this story in Matthew 4. At one point in the story, after taking Jesus to the peak of a very high mountain and showing Jesus the never-ending kingdoms at display, the devil said, "I will give it all to you."

Jesus then said, "Get out of here, Satan." Jesus goes on to say, "You must worship the Lord your God and serve Him only."

If the Devil tried to do this with Jesus, you're not immune to his deceitful practices! The enemy loves to attack us when we're most vulnerable. When you're sad, tired, lonely, angry, hurt…you're vulnerable.

The enemy is a mastermind at overpromising results. However, he has proven to underdeliver on those promises time and time again. The enemy doesn't care about you. He only wants to destroy you. He wants to see you miserable and defeated. He is the mastermind of selling lies and deception. The enemy wants you destroyed. He wants to put shackles and chains on you and leave it. But he does this with enticement at first. He lures you in.

He'll say something stupid like this: "Come on, you're entitled to disregard God's word here after all that you've been through."

"You're entitled to a little break. Treat yourself to the pleasures of sin. Just this one time."

I remember once hearing a preacher say, "The enemy doesn't give you the chain and say, 'Put it on.'" He went on to say, "No, the enemy gives you one link at a time that eventually becomes a chain on you." Those links are all those moments where the enemy overpromises things that he can't deliver on.

Here's the thing: you and I were created to worship and long after our Creator. It means that our God can truly and totally satisfy the longing that's within us. Worship is a twenty-four-hour ordeal, and we are always worshiping something or someone at any given moment. When we're not worshiping God, it's something or someone else. When it's not God, it's an idol; it's that which is antithetical to who God is.

The enemy wants this. God says, "Put your trust in Him and the plans He has for you." The enemy says, "Put your trust in yourself and listen to your own conscience." This is a very loud voice when you're going through those dark seasons. Temptations will abound but will only lead to destruction. Run away from the course of the enemy and run to God even when you don't have things figured out. Run to God even when the people around you are giving you counsel to doubt God's goodness in the midst of suffering.

The enemy loves dark seasons. He knows that if he can get permission to attack you, you'll be most prone to question the goodness of God in your life. He did this with Job! He said, "Well, duh, Job is a blameless man. Because everything in life is going great!"

When your marriage is hit hard, the enemy will say, "Just find another person, and you'll be satisfied." When the finances are crushing you, the enemy will say, "Just hit the casino with the balance of your family's 401k account. You'll win big time, and all your troubles will go away." When loneliness sets in, the enemy will say, "Just head to the strip club, and have a little fun." When the pain sinks deep in your soul, the enemy will say, "Drink the whole bottle of scotch, or take a blow." When class is burying you and you keep making low grades, the enemy will say, "Just cheat your way through to success. No one will ever know."

But, friends, the ways of the enemy will never bring lasting, true satisfaction. The grass is never greener on the other side of obedience to God, and this is so important to grasp when we already feel that we're walking on dead grass.

Allow me to share with you a season of ministry when I wanted to just give it all up and "do my own thing in life."

In 2014, I began to serve as an associate pastor at a church in Massachusetts. The church was looking for a young pastor to turn things around for them, and there was a part of me that knew there wasn't much longevity in the calling. Part of it was knowing some of their history, part of it was my youthfulness and lack of wisdom in certain areas, and part of it was the monstrosity of a task I had at hand. Yet I was intrigued and thought that if anyone could do it, it would be me.

Friend, any church that looks to you to be their savior of sorts, run away!

Don't get me wrong, there were many parts of my experience at this church that I absolutely loved, like hosting a community grilled-pizza event, starting an ESL ministry with hired ESL teachers, and starting Gospel Infusion, which was a unique church experience where we rented out a gourmet Chinese restaurant for a year and had church there! Incredible times! Those were powerful experiences for me, and it really vibed well with my passion and how my mind operated. I really loved doing new things, being innovative with ministry approaches, and piloting ministry opportunities that other people doubted could work.

But then there were experiences that were extremely difficult. I noted in the beginning of this book that I went through a season of depression at around this time, and it was because of a number of reasons. Some of it was brought upon as a result of immature decisions I've made as an associate pastor, some of it was a result of the natural hardships of pastoral ministry, and some of it was the result of God wanting to deal with sinful decisions I've made many years ago that I had not fully repented of and that I've yet to really bring to God.

What I do want to make clear is that I came to a point in my life where I sunk low. It all came to a head one day when we had one of those scheduled after-church congregational meetings to vote on the annual budget and talk about a few other agenda items. We also needed to give an update on how the former year went and propose what the new year would bring in terms of vision and mission.

After the elders gave a presentation, a family unit called me up to the front because they "had some questions" that they wanted me to respond to publicly. Of course, when none of this is planned, a level of anxiety starts to come over you, and I had no idea what to expect and what the outcome would be. Even though I tend to like change, I don't like surprises like these!

I went up to the front, not knowing what to expect.

Their first question was, "We called you as our associate pastor, so why are you not acting like one?"

"Ummm," I said. "Can you elaborate a little more on what you mean?" I asked.

"Sure can," they assured.

"Ever since you came here to *our* church, you've done nothing except bring in people from the streets who don't look like us, who don't know how things work around here, who don't even speak our language, who don't have their lives put together, and it's causing great tension among us, and you need to be held accountable," she so clearly articulated in an immaculate, loud voice for all to hear without any margin of error.

I was stunned. I was speechless, especially for someone who grew up needing to process statements and write out a response to those statements.

That started an afternoon of intense dialogue. I tend to begin my responses in a diplomatic, reasonable way, but then I grew defensive. I started to grow visibly irritable, and then I just shut down. My wife went up and grabbed me by the hands, and we just took our two children and went home. I was in such disbelief at the course of the dialogue that followed, and I was hurt. I was hurt for the manner in which they came after me, and I was hurt for all those people who came to church for the first time and were no longer welcomed there anymore. My heart grieved.

For the next several months, I sunk even lower in my emotions. I became angry and sort of hopeless.

It wasn't that much longer after that episode that I had an encounter with another family who had a problem with a certain man of color who "took" their pew that they've had for many years. Let me give you some backstory.

I went out for a walk on the streets one day, as I normally do, and I had intentions of just talking to random people. I came across this one guy that I just knew in my spirit wasn't doing well in life. When we started to talk, he spilled his guts out and started to share about the pain that was in his life. He said his brother was shot and killed just a few days prior, and he felt so hopeless. He admitted that he was so angry at God. I could smell the alcohol on his breath and knew that he turned to the bottle to deal with his issues. No judgment there. Just giving you a picture.

My heart grew for the man, and I invited him to come to church where I pastored at. I told him that I would personally save him a seat next to me and that I would walk alongside him in his journey of pain. He looked at me with curiosity and a little disbelief that I would even sit next to him. Church was the next day. After a little bit more dialogue, he departed, and I prayed that he would take my offer and come the next morning to church.

The next morning came, and I was like the father in the prodigal son story. I was looking at the horizon for this man to come, despite having a million other things on my agenda for that morning. But this man coming was more important to me than anything else.

Church was about to begin, and I grabbed a seat up front and wondered if this guy would really come.

He did! He came in, same clothes as yesterday and same breath scent, saw me, and joyfully came and sat next to me. I'll never forget the smile he had on his face when he saw that I was not kidding about my offer for him to sit next to me. I was so happy he came. For the whole service, we sat together, we sang together, he cried a lot, he sang loudly, and he said that he felt something new in him that he hadn't felt before.

Isn't that amazing! I was so excited for what was ahead. And then...

I was approached by a couple who wanted to just speak with me about something on their mind. Trying to be a good pastor, I catered to their request and listened.

The burden that they had on their heart was that this man I introduced to the church took their pew. And not only did he take their pew, but he certainly didn't fit or belong in the church because of a number of reasons, which they were so bold to tell me. I'm sure you can only imagine the reasons given. While tiptoeing around their reasons, they said, "Anyways, he's a threat to our young ladies in the church."

A threat? How?

I was shocked, but then I wasn't.

Well, in my immature personality at the time, I gathered the elders during the middle of the week, and we went into the church with our tool bags and began to dismantle almost half the front sanctuary's pews. We cut them up and disposed of them into the dumpster. Of course, I also gave a few benefits of removing the pews and had a conversation about this venture weeks ago, but this encounter with that couple gave me inspiration that the time to pull the trigger on this project was now!

When the following Sunday came, let's just say that the couple noticed their pew missing and became enraged. Actually, enraged is an understatement. Thank goodness that God was patient with me.

Did I contribute to some of the lows I was experiencing in this season of life? Yes, but hopefully not all. As I sit back and reflect on those years, I grew sad at some of the heart postures toward people who were different than the ones who rejected them.

I got to a point in my life at that time when I wanted to walk away from pastoral ministry altogether. I was underpaid (not that I was in ministry for a big pay). My wife and kids were constantly judged (like living our lives in a crystal-clear fishbowl). There was very little reward (and that's okay). I was irritable most of the time. I lacked joy. The hours were not flexible at all (at this place anyways). I lost time in some of the most formative years of my first-born child (I regret this). I was treated harshly at times and wondered if I should just walk away from the calling that God has put on my life. I was done. I wanted to throw in the towel and just pursue something else. What that was? I don't know.

I was tempted many times to live life the way I wanted and to do things that I felt would bring me satisfaction in life, but ultimately determined that striving to be obedient to God is the better way. I think, for pastors and people in ministry, the enemy waits for those moments when you feel you're failing at ministry to lure you into something "better." But when we leave God's calling on our lives for something else, there's nothing better on the other side.

Did I fail at times in striving to be obedient to God? Many, many times. Too many times, and I am so thankful that God has continued to sustain me through all those years and counting. I am so blessed that God has constantly called me back to him and has not given up on me in the moments of weakness that came in seasons when I was down in the trenches.

Now Job was the type of person that we all should attempt to be like, especially when it came to his character. Look at what the beginning of his story tells us: "He was blameless— man of complete integrity. He feared God and stayed away from evil. He had seven sons and three daughters. He owned seven thousand sheep, three thousand camels, five hundred teams of oxen, and five hundred female donkeys. He also had many servants. He was in fact, "the richest person in that entire area" (Job 1:1b–3).

Okay, maybe I don't strive to have seven thousand sheep and three thousand camels. Where would I put them all? Goats? Absolutely! But his integrity is something I envy, particularly when he pursued it as his world was being completely dismantled.

It seems like Job was living the standard life of what it would mean to be completely obedient to God. As a result of his obedience, he was blessed by God.

One day, Satan, who is noted as the "Accuser," challenges God's statement that Job is a man of integrity and is blameless. Satan basically says, "Well, no duh, of course he's obedient to you. Job has had it easy in life and has never really been through many trials and tribulations."

In a sense, I totally get that. Isn't it easier to follow God and get involved in church and praise Him when life is going our way? Let's be honest here. That was Satan's line of reasoning here. So God basically responds by saying, "Alright, you may do whatever you like to Job, but you aren't to harm him." Then Satan leaves the presence of God.

First thing I notice is this: Satan cannot do anything except by that which God allows. Why God allows it? I do not know, but God is confident that Job will be able to withstand the trials that are coming his way. God is confident that Job is a man of integrity even when sorrows and tragedies hit his life. Let's find out.

First, Job finds out that all his animals were stolen and that all his farmhands were killed. The Sabeans came in and did all this. The Sabeans were a group of people from southwest Arabia, were a rival nation to Israel, lived where it is currently recognized as Yemen, and thrived as a nation from about 1200 BC to AD 275, when a civil war destroyed their land.

Next, while the news broke to Job about the oxen and donkeys being stolen, he finds out that a fire from above came down and burned up all the sheep and the attending shepherds. Within a moment of that news, a third messenger comes in and announces that three bands of Chaldeans (people from the region north of the Persian Gulf) came in and stole all the camels and killed Job's servants.

My goodness, when it rains, it pours! This is already so much for Job to take in, yet there is more.

Another messenger came in and announced that a storm hits the house. The house collapsed and killed all his children! Job tore his robe in grief.

Let's pause right there. I don't know if I could ever go through what Job went through at this point in his life. I can't imagine losing your children—all ten of them in the case of Job. Not only did Job lose his children, but he lost them in a tragic manner. I'm going to be honest here and confess that I am not sure that I would be able to recover if I lost my kids.

Let me share with you something that happened in February of 2022. My wife was in pain all night long. Actually, she experienced stomach pain for a few days prior, but on this particular night, she was in so much pain that she couldn't even get up from the floor. I knew that something was wrong.

This was a woman who has an extremely high pain tolerance. After a very rough night for her, I decided that an ambulance was needed. The weather outside was terrible. It was sleeting ice, and that ice was accumulating fast. We had the kids home, and I knew that she needed to go to the hospital.

She was at the hospital all day long, and I was to be with the kids. She needed me to be the strong one for the kids, and I struggled with this. I had no idea what was happening. There were moments throughout the day when I cried in private because I didn't know if she was going to come home. I seriously thought that I was going to lose her, and this is a feeling that I dread. I started to wrestle with God and wondered how I could lift my hands in worship of Him if he took her.

Here I am struggling to worship God at the thought of losing my wife, and Job worshipped God when he actually loses all ten of his kids!

Now, thankfully, my wife did come home that night, and I was so emotionally overwhelmed.

What she went through that night was serious, and there was a high chance of losing her. As it turned out, she had what is called an ectopic pregnancy, where a pregnancy had gotten stuck in one of her fallopian tubes and caused it to rupture. By the time they had managed to get her into surgery, they had to drain over a liter of blood from her abdomen. With that said, we miscarried, and this would be our second miscarriage.

And miscarriages are tragic to any couple.

I remember years prior when she had miscarried, and I wasn't sure how I would react. The news was broken to us in the doctor's office. I was silent. I was not quite sure how to process it. We got in the car, and as I was driving away, I broke down crying as the car was moving. Victoria got me to stop the car and put it in the park position. We just wept in the parking lot of the doctor's office.

It took a bit of time to process all this. I know that many women suffer through these, and it absolutely wrecks them for a number of reasons. The emotional toll it can take on both the father and mother can be devastating. But I also know, without minimizing the pain of these moments, that we will be united with those precious ones we've lost one day.

Alright, back to Job.

You know what Job did when he received the news? He tore up his robe in grief, then he worshiped God and said,

> I came naked from my mother's womb, and I will be naked when I leave. The Lord gave me what I had, and the Lord has taken it away. Praise the name of the Lord.

Job worshipped God through the tragedies that fell on him, and the Bible tells us in Job 1:22 that "in all of this, Job did not sin by blaming God."

Now there is so much commentary we could dive into when it comes to the first chapter of Job alone, but it isn't within the scope of this book to cover all the areas one could possibly cover. The main focus here is that Job still decided to praise God, trust God, obey God, and follow God when life got really difficult.

This is hard! We must take time as we read this story of Job to really feel the pain that Job feels. Praising God for Job doesn't mean that he was waking up each morning singing joyfully while making chocolate chip pancakes. It was a decision Job made as he walked through the valley.

And this is something you need to hear. It is okay to have the emotions you have and to allow God to hold you. It's okay if the timeline of your processing these emotions doesn't align with the timeline that others expect of you.

We get into the second chapter of Job, and it appears that Satan isn't done yet. Satan then, after God amends the restrictions to not take Job's life, strikes Job with terrible boils all over his body. Job's wife comes onto the scene and pressures Job to curse God for allowing all this happen. Job responds to his wife by saying, "You talk like a foolish woman. Should we accept only good things from the hand of God and never anything bad?" (Job 2:10).

Most of us today, albeit in our human tendencies, would perfectly understand had Job responded differently. At this point in the story, Job is in deep anguish. In Job 2:13, it tells us that "no one said a word to Job, for they saw that his suffering was too great for words." His friends barely recognized Job from a distance because his suffering took a toll on his body.

And then we get to chapter 3 in the story, and we read that Job said, "Let the day of my birth be erased, and the night I was conceived. Let that day be turned to darkness. Let it be lost even to God on high and let no light shine on it" (Job 3:3–4). Job's birthday was no longer a celebration to him. He wished he was never born.

With the story of Job's life being so long, allow me to just lay out a few statements from Job that I think really does a good job painting us a picture of the pain and grief that Job was going through.

> If my misery could be weighed and my troubles be put on the scales, they would outweigh all

> the sands of the sea. That is why I spoke impulsively. (Job 6:2–3)

> Why won't you leave me alone, at least long enough for me to swallow! (Job 7:19)

> What do you gain by oppressing me? Why do you reject me, the work of your own hands, while smiling on the schemes of the wicked? (Job 10:3)

> I was living quietly until he shattered me. He took me by the neck and broke me to pieces. Then he set me up as his target. (Job 16:12)

> And now my life seeps away. Depression haunts my days. (Job 30:16)

These are just a few statements from Job as he is going back and forth in dialogue with his so-called friends. His friends are trying to make sense of all the pain and struggles that Job is going through. They even try to attribute it to some sin that Job has done, and we find out that just isn't true. Most of the time, we just don't have answers from why God allows us to go through seasons of despair and sorrow. But what we do know is this: let's not automatically assume that all our suffering is because we did something wrong. While there are times that we can certainly bring upon us grief by decisions we make, most suffering in the world is senseless and a result of the pure fallenness of humanity.

It's quite interesting to see that, after thirty-seven chapters of Job dialoguing with his friends, God finally responds to Job, asking him a series of many questions, which Job could not answer. And when we read these questions, we are humbled and then are made aware that, even in the midst of our struggles, our view and perspective of things is limited. Are we able to somehow trust that God's ways are better than our ways?

In the middle of God confronting him, Job even said, "I have said too much already. I have nothing more to say" (40:5). But God wasn't done yet. God said, "Brace yourself like a man, because I have some questions for you, and you must answer them" (Job 40:7). God even went on to challenge Job's ability to catch a leviathan. While we are not entirely sure what this was, what we do know is that it's a gigantic, monstrous sea creature. God goes on and challenges Job to catch one of these beasts and subdue it. Can Job do it? Well, of course not! Job is put in his place and is humbled immediately.

At the end of the book of Job, God restores Job completely after he rebukes Job's three friends for contributing to the suffering Job was going through. God restores Job's fortunes and even doubles all the animals he had at first! God even gave Job seven more sons and three more daughters! Job lived to be 140 years old and was able to see four generations of his children and grandchildren. Then he died.

As mentioned before, time and space isn't allotted here to go through all the intricacies of the story of Job in its entirety.

As difficult as it can be at times, we are called to trust God and this is a calling for us even when we're going through dark seasons. If we really think about it, what other greater option is there? Will God restore us after going through our seasons of darkness as he did for Job? I don't know. I know that for some, there is no earthly restoration. I know that for some, many, many years have passed since tragic seasons, and they are still feeling the pain. Time doesn't always heal wounds. I know that for some, they've gone through terrible things in life, and they have gotten to a point in life where they honestly do feel blessed.

What I do know is this: if we can hold fast to our trust in who God is, what He has done, and what He has said, there is a restorative reward on the other side of eternity that is no match for what we could possibly wish for this side of eternity.

I know this may sound like a quick cop-out, but it isn't. I thought that for a long time too. But when we put life into perspective, we will understand that our life is merely a parenthesis in a book of eternity.

Revelation 21:4 says, "He will wipe away every tear from their eyes, and death shall be no more, neither shall there be mourning, nor crying, nor pain anymore, for the former things have passed away." Isn't that amazing!

Listen, I know that this is all easier to talk about than to grasp onto when we're going through seasons of loss, depression, and grief. I totally get that. But I pray that you'll store up these truths somewhere in the depths of your soul and go to them every time the enemy starts to sow words of condemnation and lies as you go through trials. When you hear the enemy speak absolute nonsense, you say to him, "Listen, you're on borrowed time, and your time is almost up."

There is also another truth in this story: it's in how we respond to those going through these dark seasons. Sometimes, we just need to shut our mouths for we can contribute to their suffering when we say unnecessary things. Sometimes we just need to sit in silence with them, hold them, hug them, and be there for them. Oftentimes, there isn't a correct answer we can give to those who've lost their child in a tragic school shooting, or lost their loved ones to an overdose, or lost their loved ones killed by someone else.

There are situations that are simply just messy beyond our comprehension, but somehow, God is in the midst of it all. Somehow, we can trust God that our suffering doesn't have the final say.

James 5:11 says, "Behold, we consider those blessed who remained steadfast. You have heard of the steadfastness of Job, and you have seen the purpose of the Lord, how the Lord is compassionate and merciful."

It is hard to praise God in the storm, but let's aim to do so.

So what's the big takeaway here? When life throws you lemons, make lemonade. Just kidding. No, when life gets difficult, run to God, not away. Be honest with God. Often, I say to God, "I'm going through some difficult stuff right now, and I'm going to need your help worshiping you." I think you'll be amazed when you pray this prayer.

For the church, teach the people how to be people of integrity even when one doesn't feel like doing the right thing. Integrity isn't always emotional. It's a decision that we will praise God in the storm.

It's a decision to look back at how much grace God gives us when we don't deserve it. Our Sunday morning services may be emotionally uplifting but you need to allow people time to process, venture through their stuff in life, and heal. An hour isn't going to do it.

I would also say this: your expectation of how God ought to heal another individual oftentimes won't match reality. Don't be like Job's friends here. Just sit in silence and journey with your friend.

CHAPTER 4

Esther
(Invisible to Others)

One of the things I love about what Jesus does throughout the Gospels is that He makes people who feel invisible seen. He makes them known, and He makes them heard. And as I reflect on what that means, I've come to the realization that people who struggle with depression don't see themselves as seen by those around them. They feel invisible; that no one really cares about who they are. Not only do they feel invisible, but they sense a deep contempt toward them. When this happens, they are either pushed to the fringes of society, or there is a desire from people to see them wiped away from the face of the earth, like what happened to Jewish people under Hitler, and to black men and women in the Jim Crow South.

But let's press the matter a little bit harder. Not only is there an ongoing issue with groups of people who feel invisible because of the color of their skin, but we see this very thing among the special needs community, those who struggle with addictions, victims of human trafficking, kids in the foster care system, and so forth. If we can think about this for just a moment, we come to the realization that when you are systematically targeted due to whatever reason, you begin to buy into this idea that your life holds no intrinsic value. Why? Because you've been conditioned to think this way by the way people around you treat you.

In this chapter, I want to take us through the entire story of Esther, who was faced with the possible extermination of her race. Before we do that, let me bring us to the story of Jesus and his encounter with Zacchaeus.

In Luke's Gospel, we're told that Jesus was taking a stroll through the town of Jericho, and there was a man there by the name of Zacchaeus. It tells us that Zacchaeus was the chief tax collector, so this means he was a man hated by society. In collecting taxes from the people, Zacchaeus became very rich and wealthy.

One day, he heard that Jesus was in town. He'd heard a few things about this Jesus, and he wanted to see him and check out what all the hype was about. The problem he faced was that there were too many people surrounding Jesus, and he was extremely short. So what did Zacchaeus do? He climbed a tree to get a look.

I often wonder what was going through his head at this moment. I'm sure there are a host of feelings the reader has, such as having no sympathy for the man because of how he'd treated others, but what Jesus did next challenges our stance.

When Jesus comes walking by, he looked up at Zacchaeus and he *calls him by name*. To know about someone and to know their name are two different things, and Jesus knows Zacchaeus by name despite the life he's living. Have you ever felt no one knew your name?

Growing up, I knew of many bullies in school, and I would see how they would treat the "unnamed" kid in class or the cafeteria. They would hurl insults at a certain kid, throw kicks and punches, and completely humiliate the person. They would do this over and over again and not know the name of the person they were doing this to. And one day, a group of high school students from next door came to lunch and sat down with one particular middle school kid who was bullied and allowed no one to bully this kid anymore.

This group of high school students asked for this kid's name, bought him new shoes, ate lunch with him the rest of the school year, protected this kid at all costs, and elevated the kid's value and dignity. They sent a message to the bullies to back off. The kid who was bullied started to feel like his life mattered because he was seen by someone else and his name was known.

You see, when your life has been reduced to a number or a stat, you don't feel very loved. As a pastor, one of the most important things I strive for is to memorize people's names as well as anyone else in their life who is immediately connected. In fact, I would really get upset at myself if I didn't remember their name on the second try. Why is this? Because there is something about having your name known that makes you feel wanted in life. My goal is to communicate that *you* are important to me and that *you* are more than just a number in a seat.

So here we have Jesus. He called Zacchaeus by name and told him to quickly come down so they can wine and dine at his house that night. Zacchaeus got down, and he took Jesus to his house. Zacchaeus was super excited. However, the people were a bit upset at this encounter. They were angry that Jesus has gone to spend time with a known sinner. In their eyes, Zacchaeus didn't deserve to be seen. He deserved to be punished, pushed to the outskirts of society.

There was an encounter between Jesus and Zacchaeus at his house that led to Zacchaeus giving back all the money to the people he cheated and stole from. Jesus even declared that salvation had come to the house of Zacchaeus.

If Jesus here is demonstrating to us that even the chief of sinners has the possibility of being seen and restored, how much more so is this true for those who are invisible to society purely based off their skin color, their race, their culture, their religion, their disabilities, and so forth? I always like to imagine that the people in society who are unable to defend themselves have a special place in the heart of God that goes into eternity. We'll explore more on this shortly.

Esther is a story that perfectly drives home our point there. For the sake of jogging our memory or introducing the story to some for the first time, and to not skip over any important details pertinent to our conversation, let's take on Esther's story chapter by chapter.

Chapter 1 opens up with King Xerxes on the scene, and he decided to host a banquet in the third year of his reign. He sent out a massive invite, and the celebration, in order to display all the wealth he had, lasted 180 days! Now, think about that for a minute. I personally think I need just an hour to display any wealth I have. The annual Macy's Thanksgiving Parade is only three hours, and there's so much there!

It takes King Xerxes 180 days to do this. Isn't that insane! It's hard to wrap my head around this.

After this celebration, he holds an elaborate banquet in which he orders each man to be served in whatever way they felt. He then orders his wife, Queen Vashti, to do a dance in front of all the men, but she refused, and this angered King Xerxes. After consulting his advisors on what should be done with her as a result of her disobedience, they suggest that Queen Vashti be banished from his presence forever and that a new woman should be made queen. They did this because they didn't want women all over the place to feel that they had license to disobey their husbands. The King took this counsel seriously and issued this decree throughout his vast empire.

Now we get to the second chapter, and it says that the king's anger subsided. Upon reflecting for a while on all that just happened, King Xerxes decided to throw a beauty pageant, and whoever caught the attention of the king's eyes would be made queen.

At this time, there was a man whose name was Mordecai, and he had a cousin who was very beautiful. Her name was Esther. Esther's parents died earlier in her life, and Mordecai raised her as his own daughter. Hegai, who was a eunuch, was placed in charge of spotting who may be the one for the King. He was impressed with Esther and made sure that she was treated highly.

I find it interesting that the text tells us that Esther was instructed by Mordecai not to make her nationality known. Over the course of the next several months, Esther was made queen, and King Xerxes "loved Esther more than any of the other young women." In the midst of all this, Mordecai was made an official in the palace. Understandably, Mordecai was constantly looking out after Esther and kept ensuring that Esther kept her nationality a secret.

Mordecai proved himself worthy when he discovered that there were two guards planning to assassinate King Xerxes and he made this known. When the king found out who these two guards were, he ordered that they be impaled on a sharpened tool. I guess that's one way to execute. Not my preferred method should I ever be so unfortunate to be terminally punished.

In the third chapter, we are introduced to Haman, who was promoted as the most powerful official in the empire. When everyone bowed down to Haman, Mordecai did not. We are not really sure why he didn't, and one can only speculate the reasons, but we know that this didn't please Haman at all. The officials decided to chat with Haman to see if this would be tolerated, and I find it also interesting that the story tells us that Mordecai told the officials he was Jewish. I often wonder why he did this when he instructed Esther to remain quiet. Did he do this in a casual conversation, and it sort of slipped out? I do not know. But now it'll be used against him.

When Haman found out that Mordecai didn't bow down to him and when he found out that he was also Jewish, Haman became enraged and began to plot the extermination of all Jewish people throughout the entire empire of King Xerxes.

Haman had a chat with the king and began to facilitate a story that was so off base and bent the truth in more ways than one. Long story short, he got the king to order a decree to dispose of a "certain group of people" who were "deliberate in disobeying the king's orders." As a result, Haman was able to dispatch people throughout the empire to slaughter, kill, and annihilate all Jewish people, including women and children. There was going to be weeping and wailing throughout all the cities, and cries would be too much for the ears to handle.

Chapter 4 comes, and Mordecai was horrified at what happened. I wonder what's going through his head. Not only was he mortified at the decree, but I wonder if he felt that his actions had brought this on. He let Queen Esther know what was happening, and it tells us that Queen Esther was "deeply distressed."

To be distressed means that something has upset or worried you. When one does a quick Google search, you'll find that other words for *deeply distressed* include "much-dreaded," "terrified," "petrified," "frightened," "horrified," and so forth. This is a deep-seated emotion and rightly so. It's even more so when the person you're distressed about happens to be the man who took you in as his daughter.

Queen Esther ordered Hathach, another eunuch in the palace, to find out what was really happening to Mordecai because she wasn't exactly sure. Her instincts told her it was serious. She just knew that something bad was bothering Mordecai. Mordecai told Hathach what happened and asked Hathach to beg Queen Esther to tell King Xerxes what was happening. Of course, there is fear because no one can approach the king without being invited or they will be killed immediately on the spot. Everyone, by that point, knows that the king has a hot temper.

Mordecai told Esther that she must speak up for her people and warned her not to think that she was protected from this decree simply because she's a queen. Queen Esther then ordered all the Jewish people to fast for her. She then took a risk and accepted that she might die. She went in to see the king.

Chapter 5 comes, and Esther approached the king. Of course, the king welcomed her, and he was head over heels for Esther and even granted any request she may have by saying that she could even have half the kingdom! Queen Esther was going to put on a banquet and wanted the king and Haman to come. She said, "Just come to the banquet tomorrow, and I'll explain to you what all this is about."

Haman learned of the invite and started to brag to those around him about it. In the midst of all this, he still came across Mordecai at the gates and got so angry at Mordecai that he planned to assassinate him. Haman ordered a seventy-five-foot sharpened pole to be hoisted so he could ask the king to impale Mordecai. Why seventy-five feet? I do not know. Seems a bit dramatic if you ask me.

In chapter 6, the king had a hard time sleeping, so he ordered a book to be read to him (kids, this doesn't mean that books are only produced to make you fall asleep). In this book, he found out about how Mordecai prevented an assassination attempt on the king! The king then wanted to know what had been done to reward this man. But nothing had been done. He then asked Haman what could be done to honor a man who truly pleases him. Haman, in his total ignorance, told the king how such a man should be honored. The king liked Haman's suggestions and ordered this to be done. When he learned that the man to be honored was Mordecai, he became quickly humiliated.

Now it was time for the banquet. In chapter 7, Queen Esther made it known about the man who plotted to completely wipe away all the Jewish people, her people. "Who would do such a thing?!" asked the king.

Queen Esther said, "Well, Haman is the culprit here." The king got so angry. Haman went before Esther to plead with her to spare his life. In doing so, he fell onto Esther's couch, and the king came rushing in and saw Haman on his beloved wife's couch! Oh, this angered the king even more, for this wasn't a good picture. He even accused Haman of potentially assaulting his wife. The king ordered Haman to be taken away and impaled on the seventy-five-foot pole Haman intended to use to impale Mordecai. What a gruesome death! When Haman was impaled, the king's anger subsided.

In chapter 8, Esther pleaded with the king to overturn the decree that the king was manipulated into issuing. Until a decree was overturned, the Jewish people were not safe. King Xerxes overturned the decree and vowed to protect the Jewish people out of great love for Esther. They would now be protected and no longer faced with annihilation. The book of Esther ends by highlighting how famous Mordecai had become. The Jewish people even inaugurated a yearly celebration of this victory, known as Purim.

Purim is the ancient word for "casting lots." Haman cast lots to determine the exact date when the Jewish people were to be completely wiped out. The plan, of course, backfired, and they decided to call the celebration "Purim" as a way of signifying how the plans of the enemy were turned upside down; thwarted.

Whew. And that's the story of Esther in a nutshell.

If you go back and reread the story and just sort of soak it all in, try to fill in the blanks. So often, we read stories like this in the Bible and just move on while getting the main point. I often like to insert myself into the major characters of the story to get a feel for what was going on. For example, what was it like to be Mordecai? How many sleepless nights did he have in the midst of a death threat from the most powerful man in the province? He feared for his life.

Then what feelings were going through him when the decree went out? When we read about the potential extermination of the Jewish people, we need to remember that little kids would be slaughtered on that day and that moms would watch in horror, unable to protect their babies, and then get killed afterward. The scene would be horrifying.

Did Mordecai feel guilty? Not that any of this was his fault, but one could imagine how sick to your stomach you would be for letting your nationality slip out in conversation, whether intentional or not. If I were in his shoes, I'd like to imagine that I would plead with Haman to only kill me and spare my people.

One can only imagine the feelings that Esther had. Let's talk about this.

First, we know that Esther was an orphan. I mean, thank goodness that Mordecai took her in as his own! But it is never easy knowing that your parents died. It wasn't easy back then and it's not easy today.

My father left before I was even born. My mother had to give me up to the foster care system. Today, I have a man in my life whom I call Dad. He came into my life when I was a middle schooler, and I am so thankful for him. Yet there is always going to be a part of you that wishes for a "normal" experience. You wish your kids had another set of grandparents. You wish you had parents who could have taught you the things that would be so valuable today. You start to wonder what is wrong with "me" that my parents left. It's always there in the back of your mind.

And I can't imagine what it would be like to lose your parents before you've really only begun life. I can only imagine the ups and downs in your emotions. This was Esther, a young girl without mom or dad and having to go through all that life would throw at her without them.

Second, even with customs being the way they were back then, Esther was taken advantage of. I know we don't like talking about these types of things, but I'm going to call it what it is. In the second chapter of Esther, we read this:

> Before each young woman was taken to the
> king's bed, she was given the prescribed twelve

> months of beauty treatments—six months with oil of myrrh, followed by six months with special perfumes and ointments. When it was time for her to go to the king's palace, she was given her choice of whatever clothing or jewelry she wanted to take from the harem. That evening she was taken to the king's private rooms, and the next morning she was brought to the second harem, where the king's wives lived. There she would be under the care of Shaashgaz, the king's eunuch in charge of the concubines. She would never go to the king again unless he had especially enjoyed her and requested her by name. (Esther 2:12–14)

Yes, this is exactly what you are imagining it says. The king basically calls in a group of virgin girls and sleeps with them all, one by one. When he's had a night with them, he would send the girls out to the second harem, most likely never to be seen again by the king. It was a walk of shame for most of them. With all the preparations the girls took for their beauty, the king could easily "use" them and then "dispose" of them. The king took away their virginity and left them vulnerable. In those times, it would take a miracle for them to find a husband who would want them despite their virginity being taken away.

Now am I being a bit too harsh here with what happened? No, I am not. Sometimes, we tend to skip over these parts and pretend they are not there. Do you really think Esther and those girls could just refuse to service the king? Of course not! They would be killed. They didn't have a choice in the matter. If they wanted a chance to live, they must do what the king wanted, even all his sexual fantasies.

The king abused his position of authority, whether this was normal custom or not. Can you imagine being one of those girls and being used like this? Can you imagine the shame you had to carry with you the rest of your life? Now, you might say, "Yeah, but Esther was the lucky one who caught the eyes of the king." True, but there is a big difference between the king being in love with her and the king being "in lust" with her. Queen Esther was still only property to the king.

Third, not only was Esther orphaned, but she was culturally homeless. The story takes place after the Babylonian exile. With permission given, the Jewish people could either stay and live as cultural foreigners throughout Persia, or they could actually go back home to Jerusalem. The problem was that Jerusalem was torn apart by war. What would you choose?

I often talk to families who immigrate to the United States in search of a better life. It's interesting to hear their perspective. Could they have chosen to stay behind or to go back if life was difficult in the States for them? Sure, oftentimes, they would be going back to a land run by warlords, terrorist groups, etc. On the same side of the coin, I often meet families who are so worn down by being in the States because they are often abused by the people here in the States. To them, what were they going to do? Report them? It was a citizen's word against a foreigner.

On top of all this, there is the language barrier for these families and them having to navigate difficult cultural landscapes without their family. That can get extremely lonely.

Esther was in a land that was not really hers. She was homeless at home.

Fourth, even being the queen, she risked her life when Mordecai wanted Esther to make known to Xerxes the decree that put all their lives at risk. She needed permission to appear before the king or she risked death. We already know that the king had a temper that easily could do serious harm and damage to those around him.

Fifth, her people were at severe risk of being exterminated. This was no light matter here. Think about the Jewish people under Hitler. Think about black people during slavery and the Jim Crow South. Think about the Cambodians who were killed under the Khmer Rouge. Think about the Armenians under the Ottoman Empire. Think about Tutsis in Rwanda. There are so many more examples throughout history, and there's so much of that happening today. It's evil. When you and your people are at risk of being slaughtered, you feel invisible. You feel that you have no intrinsic worth. You feel that you don't belong.

Esther was at risk for all this, even being the queen. All these five things are more than enough to force a person to experience the deep ebb and flows of depression. Now, thankfully, there is a great ending in the story of Esther in which the Jewish people claimed victory, but present victory doesn't just erase past calamity.

As I venture through the story of Esther, I am reminded of all the people today who are "invisible" to society. It is argued that there are more than forty million modern-day slaves and most of our American society is built and is operated on the back of this evil enterprise. It's such a hidden ordeal yet right in front of our faces. And the tempting thing to do is to ignore it; to not think too much of it. We think, "As long as I'm not aware of it, then it's fine." We think, "As long as attention isn't brought to the realities of it, then I'm not complicit." Yet Jesus, one day, will bring justice for these people. I stand by the conviction that God has a very special place for people who are abused, trafficked, and neglected.

I think about the people we pass on the streets. Whether it was their decision or not that landed them on the streets, they still have names and stories. They still are someone's daughter and son. At one point in their lives, they were sweet, innocent children. Maybe drugs got the worst of them. Maybe they aged out of the foster care system. I don't know, but I do know that Christ laid His life down for them too.

I think about the elderly who live in nursing homes and don't have anyone to visit them. They just sort of sit in those homes waiting for their lives to expire. There isn't anyone to love them. I've visited a number of nursing homes, and my heart breaks, especially for those placed in homes by able children who rarely visit them because life got busy. I can imagine they feel invisible. I can imagine they feel depressed and heartbroken. I can imagine the tears they shed each night.

I think about the mentally ill. We sort of just section them off to a slice of society, and we "pray" they get better. We adopt the mentality that as long as they are managed and controlled, then we can get by in tolerating them.

I think about our veterans who come home from military life and are no longer seen as heroes. Many of our vets become homeless, commit suicide, and have an extremely difficult time adapting to normal life here in the States.

I think about those in prison. We may think that they deserve to be in there, and yet that is such a complicated statement. How many people in our prison system are there by way of fair justice? How many are wrongfully convicted? How many need to be in rehab and not in a punitive ward? And didn't Jesus say something about visiting the people in prison? For most, it's out of sight, out of mind.

There are so many groups of people I can think of right now who feel invisible, and this can lead to a life that they don't desire to live, but there is one more group of people I want to talk about that's near and dear to my heart. It's the special needs community.

First, let me share with you some context. Victoria (my wife) and I have five children. Three have come by way of natural birth. The other two are adopted. Two of my kids, plus myself, wear hearing aids. One wears glasses. One of my kids was a drug baby, and there could be a chance that he will experience the side effects of that reality as he ages.

One of my children came to live with us when she was just shy of four years old. She isn't able to eat by way of mouth, isn't able to talk audibly in a way that people understand, isn't able to dance, isn't able to do a whole lot of things, and the crazy thing is that she could do all of these things her first couple of years of her life. Rae is a precious, sweet little girl who, unfortunately, experienced traumatic brain injury due to a voluntary, tragic incident when she was so little.

Since being with us for almost a couple of years, she has made so much progress. Her smile is contagious, and she is learning very slowly how to take a few bites of soft food and is talking nonstop (although it isn't in the way you and I talk). While she has made progress, she has a long road ahead of her. Will she ever fully recover? I do not know. She became my miracle in shaping my heart, desires, and passion for people like her.

When we first found out about her, the story was a bit sad. She was receiving "care," but only the basic care. Enough care to keep her alive. Yet what about being nurtured? What about lifting the drugs from her that would lift the fog that clouded her beautiful personality?

When she came to live with us, we became committed to doing everything we could to give this little girl the best life that was stolen from her. The longer we have her, the more we are made aware of how much of a "bother" or a "nuisance" special needs people are to others in our society. They take up a lot of time, a lot of resources, a lot of energy, and they slow down the everyday gears of life for "normal" people. We've heard so many ignorant comments about her and other special needs people that it's astounding. We've heard stories of special needs children being mistreated in the school system, and for those who are nonverbal, it's scary. They can't speak up for themselves, and they can't communicate with us when something bad happens to them. The special needs community is one of the biggest "hand over mouth" smothered groups of people.

Now I am very much pleased that we've made lots of progress in this area as a society, but there is a difference between awareness and action. Society isn't built for special needs. The special needs community are some of the most precious individuals and deserve as much care as we can provide for them. Most, if not all these people, are the way that they are not by any fault of their own. Some were born that way, some were taken advantage of, some were abused, some were thrown into this reality by way of an accident or a biological happening. Either way, Proverbs 31:8–9 tells us to "speak up for those who cannot speak for themselves; ensure justice for those being crushed. Yes, speak up for the poor and helpless, and see that they get justice."

At the time of this writing, I was watching one of my favorite shows with my wife and two oldest girls. It was *America's Got Talent*. In the current season, Season 18, there was a contestant who appeared on stage during the very early moments of *AGT*. Her name was Lavender Darcangelo. She was blind and had autism. She sang a song, and when she finished, the entire crowd was on their feet, including the judges.

She did an amazing job, and I'll confess that there were a few tears because it was absolutely beautiful to see support coming around this girl. What was even more beautiful was when one of the judges, Heidi Klum, pushed the golden buzzer, and gold confetti came falling from the skies! Heidi made it very clear that she would walk the whole way through the show with Lavender.

Now what if we dignified every special needs person in a similar way where we show them that they matter? What if we slowed down in life and took the time to talk with them, to laugh with them, to do life with them? What if we made space in society for them to integrate with all the rest of society? What if we made more playgrounds more accessible? What if we just gave a chance for these wonderful people?

Living life in a vegetative state because you received very basic, minimal care brings a person's spirits down. They want to be nurtured. They want to have someone play with them. They want someone to make the world a special place for them.

I end this chapter with a strong call for us to do all that we can to treat every human life as life created by God.

Taking in Rae was one of the best decisions we've made. Is it challenging at times? Of course, but she has been more of a miracle for us than anything. The miracle is her changing my heart. The miracle is seeing the rest of my kids learning to be kind, loving, and compassionate toward people of all skin colors and abilities. The miracle is that I get to see her smile and be reminded of God's love for her and people like her.

People who feel invisible, targeted, and marginalized don't tend to have a raging fire in them. They tend to have just a small glowing ember, and we can do so much as blessed people to enable them to see that ember grow into a raging fire of passion, purpose, and dignity with just a spark from us. And if you are someone who feels invisible, let me say this:

As victory finally came for the Jewish people in the book of Esther, there is an ultimate victory you can have in Christ. I say this because the reality is that there are so many people who don't see a worldly victory. We see this all the time, and I take comfort and find hope in the fact that Jesus will one day come back to make all things new.

Psalm 91:1–2, 4 says, "Those who live in the shelter of the Most High will find rest in the shadow of the Almighty. This I declare about the Lord: He alone is my refuge, my place of safety; He is my God, and I trust Him… He will cover you with His feathers. He will shelter you with His wings. His faithful promises are your armor and protection." This is beautiful, and I long for the day when the effects of sin are no more. I long for the day when evil will be completely eradicated. I long for the day when Jesus comes back to lift up the humble and bring them strength.

CHAPTER 5

Hannah
(Cries of Desperation)

I was in the car with my wife one day, and we were starting to pull out of the parking lot of the doctor's office we had just visited. As the car started to move, I, the driver, began to cry uncontrollably. Victoria directed me to press the brakes, and then she put the car in the parked position. We weren't even in a proper parking space, but I just couldn't keep going.

I don't generally cry in front of others often. I try to hold it in, and I certainly try to minimize when my cry is a bit dramatic. It was the type of cry that morning that was heavy, and it pressed on my soul. We had just miscarried our first baby.

Now I always knew that there is always a risk of miscarriage, and it is more common than one thinks, but nothing really prepares you for the moment when it happens. You think you're strong enough, but you are not. It certainly didn't help that the sky was overcast. We held each other in our arms the rest of the day, and most of the day was spent in silence. What words would we even say?

I don't exactly remember the thoughts that were going through my head, but I do remember asking God, "Why?" Why did this have to happen? Why did the dream just die? What did we do to deserve this? Don't you care about the little ones? Aren't you capable of all things? Why all the excitement and buildup just to have it all crushed in a moment? What was next?

And I remember being so distracted. I was in college, and those immediate days following the news were a bit difficult. I couldn't focus. For me, it does take a while to get out of my slump. People were asking me what the matter was. To be honest, I thought I hid it well. I didn't really speak about it. They would say that I was not myself, which is easily understandable when you go from 0 to 60 in an instant.

I was the kid on campus with a raging amount of energy. I was excited about everything, and I was a bit hyper. I was always loud, always jumping around, always making jokes, always laughing, always playing with others, always smiling, but not that week. I was down.

And it's in those moments when we are drawn super close to God. We bring our desperation to Him because we realize just how weak we are inside. We realize just how out of control of life we are. We realize we need some greater strength than we thought was in us. We need Him, and one of the things God allows us to do is to run to Him with the heaviness. My heart was heavy that week.

I didn't feel like talking to anyone. I didn't feel like staying up late. I didn't feel like laughing and doing extracurricular activities that week. I just felt like being sad and wondering if any hope was left down the road. Maybe you're thinking, "Oh come on, that's a bit dramatic. It happens more often than not." Sure, but when it happens to *you*, it takes a bit of time to just "get over."

I want to share here a portion of the life of Hannah, the mother of the prophet Samuel. In no way do I claim that our experience that morning and that week resonates with the story of Hannah. At least not in this instance. There have been other instances in my life that do resonate, and I'll share in a little bit, but the point I want to make here is that seasons of desperation can be somehow redeemed.

The story of Hannah is found in the first chapter of 1 Samuel. The story opens up by letting us know that there was a man named Elkanah, and Elkanah had two wives. Their names were Peninnah and Hannah.

Each year, Elkanah would travel to the temple to offer sacrifices. During that time, Hophni and Phinehas were the priests in charge. While there, Elkanah would give portions of the meat to Peninnah and her children, but he would give only one choice portion to Hannah. Why? Though he loved Hannah, God had not given Hannah children. The text tells us that God kept her from having children.

Each year when this pilgrimage took place, Peninnah would taunt Hannah about this ordeal, and this taunting would bring Hannah to tears, and she wouldn't eat.

And then her husband would ask, "Why are you crying and why aren't you eating?" And then he says something pretty stupid in my estimation. He says, "Why be downhearted just because you have no children? You have me—isn't that better than having ten sons?"

I keep rereading this statement by Elkanah, and I keep getting a bit irritated because it sort of lacks a sensitivity level toward his wife. First, I don't think guys know what it feels like to want a child and to not be able to have one. Second, there's more to life for a woman than her husband. What I mean by this is that Hannah has every right to be extremely sad at the situation at hand.

It's like me saying to my wife, "Why are you so sad that you lost your dream job? You have me. Isn't that enough?" Or something like this. Empathy definitely isn't a strong suit here. Can he not understand that, not only is Hannah unable to have a child, but she is taunted by her husband's other wife. That has to be a terrible feeling to have, and I feel terrible for Hannah at this point in the story.

As the story continues, it tells us that Hannah got up to go pray. Eli, who was a priest and also the father of Hophni and Phinehas from earlier, was sitting right there within earshot of Hannah. In verse 10, we read that "Hannah was in deep anguish, crying bitterly as she prayed to the Lord." A quick Google search online will tell us *anguish* is defined as "extreme pain, distress, or anxiety." This is desperation because Hannah is deeply wounded. In those times, it was a sign of God's lack of favor on a woman if she couldn't give birth.

Hannah approaches the throne of God and makes a "deal" with the Lord. "If you should so bless me with a child, I'll dedicate him to you for his entire life." She is pleading with God. She is pleading with God to hear her. And as she is praying, the priest noticed that her mouth was moving but no words were heard by him. He comes bursting in and says, "Are you drunk?" Of course, Hannah is a bit taken back by this and assures Eli that she is not. She makes it known to him that she is pouring her heart out to the Lord, for she has been praying out of great anguish and sorrow.

Eli then says, "In that case, go in peace!" He even says, "May the God of Israel grant the request you have asked of him." What a beacon of hope that Hannah now has for the priest to say this. After he said this, she went back to eating again, and she was no longer sad. In that moment, she took on a whole other level of faith and took Eli's word as gospel.

As time goes by, we are told that God remembered Hannah's plea, and she eventually gave birth to a little boy named Samuel. Hannah fulfilled her promise to God and ended up bringing Samuel, when he's weaned, to Eli at the temple. To be weaned back then meant that a little one had begun to develop "personhood." A big sign of this was when a child began making tangible decisions.

She was at the temple and basically says to Eli, "Remember me from several years back? The Lord granted me my request, and I am here to give him to the Lord for his entire life." The story does continue on, but I want to end it there for the purpose of our conversation.

Hannah was deeply wounded, and as I read her story, I am reminded of Psalm 34:17–18, which says, "The Lord hears his people when they call to him for help. He rescues them from all their troubles. The Lord is close to the brokenhearted; he rescues those whose spirits are crushed."

Can you remember a time when your spirit was crushed? As a pastor, I encounter numerous people who have their spirits crushed, and there is this level of despair that they can't imagine they'll get through. They have no other choice but to bring it to God and have hope that God will be there for them.

I have encountered a few people this year alone who have gone through incredibly difficult divorce situations, and they get pretty messy. As I listen to the stories, my heart breaks. My heart breaks for the family whose father just walked out on them and showed no sign of ever coming back. My heart breaks for the husband whose wife just up and left and took away the kids, making it near impossible for the husband to have access to those kids. Of course, there is always more to the story than one hears, but the story is tragic when a breakup occurs and the kids suffer as a result.

My heart breaks for the parents who lost their little one to gun violence or to suicide. My heart breaks for the little girl whose puppy was just hit by a car and died. My heart breaks for the family who has to watch their little boy go through the horrific journey of leukemia.

When I was in high school, I had to take a Bible class, and my teacher was one of the best teachers I've ever had. He was a US Marine guy, and he made Bible class extra enjoyable. His personality was contagious. Everyone loved this teacher, and I got to spend two years under his leadership.

He was also a guy who had a growing family. To be honest, I lost track of how many kids he had, and he always seemed to enjoy the craziness of a big, growing family. And then one day, after a few weeks when things were sort of "off" with one of his little girls and after much testing, he received the news that his little girl was terminally ill. There was nothing the doctors could do. There was no cure. All that could be done was to bring this little girl home and love her as much as possible until the day she passed away.

My teacher took this extremely hard, as any loving dad would. He loved her intensely, but he also wrestled with God and begged God to spare her life. He had many sleepless nights, many intense nights, and many nights when he was in deep anguish. Sadly, the little girl, despite all the prayers offered, passed away, and this has led to my teacher walking away from the faith altogether.

Now I don't know why little children die and the wicked ones live. I don't know the mystery behind all this. I don't have answers that'll satisfy, but what I do know is that little girl will one day be reunited with her family again.

I went to the funeral with my wife, and I just didn't have words for him. I cried with him, and he looked me in the eye and asked, with tears in his, "B, why is God so quick to help people find their car keys but so silent in the final moments of my child's life?"

Gosh, life can suck sometimes, can't it?

I can imagine that my teacher spent many moments like that of Hannah. And it seems like those moments, those seasons, are so unbearable and so long. No matter what we do, we keep waking up, and the nightmare continues.

I mentioned before that I don't have all the answers as to why God allows certain things to happen, but I can bring you to a moment when Jesus experienced the deep anguish that Hannah experienced and that my teacher experienced.

In those final moments of Jesus's life, we find him in what's called the Garden of Gethsemane. He's with his disciples, the Last Supper has already happened, Judas has already agreed to betray Jesus, and the plot to kill Jesus is underway. In the Gospel of Matthew, we see that Jesus is right there in the garden, and he asks the disciples to go over "there" to pray. He then takes a few of the disciples and says, "My soul is crushed with grief to the point of death. Stay here and keep watch with me."

Often, I get the honor of walking beside people in their final moments in the hospital or a nursing home. When I pray with or over a person, their hand will reach to my hand, and they would tighten their grip. With their hands shaking, they would look into my eyes and shed a tear. They just want someone to be there close with them as they cross over from life to death. Those moments are difficult, and I can imagine that Jesus is feeling this. He knows that the hour has come and he wants his disciples, his close friends, to be right there with him.

Jesus, being fully God, was also fully man and experienced the depths of what our soul experiences. Jesus bowed His head to the ground and even said, "If it is possible, let this cup of suffering be taken away from Me. Yet I want Your will to be done, not Mine." Think about that for a moment. Jesus, the Son of God, God Himself, was asking for all that was about to transpire to not happen. Of course, He wanted the will of the Father to be done. Why is this? Because He loves you and me that much. He was going to move forth with the mission He had come here to earth for, but it's important to understand that Jesus isn't some out-of-touch God that has no idea what we're going through. He has every idea because he's gone through it.

In the same story, but a different account, Luke tells us this: "He prayed more fervently, and he was in such agony of spirit that his sweat fell to the ground like great drops of blood" (Luke 22:44). Now, we may read that and think that it's crazy to sweat drops of blood, but there's an actual medical term for this, and it's called hematidrosis. This is a rare condition that happens when a person is under extreme physical or emotional stress.

I've never had this happen to me, and I haven't met anyone to whom this has happened. And to think that Jesus had this happen to Him highlights to me the agony that He was in. I'm obviously bouncing around everywhere here and sort of going between seasons of sadness, loneliness, depression, agony, duress, anxiety, and more because there are things that all those states of emotions share in common. When we're going through any of those things, our spirits are brought low.

Think about all the symptoms we've covered through the various stories of biblical characters we've talked about: loss of appetite, sadness, loss of interest in things where interest used to be, agitation, irritability, hopelessness, excessive crying, sleepiness, social isolation, fatigue, mood swings, a desire for life to just be done with already, shame, guilt, etc. These are heavy emotions, and I'm aiming to speak to those who have gone or are going through seasons where these traits are common. Truth is, it'll hit us all at some point or another and for a variety of reasons.

I think that the biggest game-changer here is whether or not we believe there's an ounce of hope left somewhere because when we think that all hope is lost, we're navigating extremely stormy waters. My yearning is to say that there is still an ounce of hope left in that small glowing ember because you're still here, hanging on. You may not be able to see any sort of brightness in the future, but I'm pleading with you to give Jesus a chance, and if you already are giving Jesus a chance, press into Him even tighter.

I know that going through seasons that are heavy are not seasons we want to be in, but there is purpose we can find. Gold cannot reach its utmost level of purity without going through extremely high levels of heat.

As I think about those nights of desperation that Hannah experienced, I'm reminded of a similar season I went through in 2005. Allow me to elaborate a little more and to provide some context first.

I surrendered my life to Jesus in December of 2004. My youth pastor (I went to youth group because it was fun, and flirting was my spiritual gift) took a large group of us to upstate New York where there would be a gigantic conference. It was something like four days long. We stayed in a pretty hotel, and it was just a solid experience.

Yes, part of me didn't want to go to some Jesus-y thing, and I didn't really have much of a choice, but a bigger part of me wanted to just get away from home, be with friends, and experience a different side of life. Honestly, I forgot if I was in Rochester, New York, or if it was Buffalo, New York, but there was so much snow! I love snow.

I had never seen so much snow in my entire life and I surely took it all in. My youth pastor explained to us that each day there would be two main sessions called Power Sessions. We would all go to an arena, which was a big dome, and be with twenty thousand other kids our age. The Power Sessions would include worship that never ended, a message that felt like a couple of hours, and a whole lot of craziness. I'm not joking. These Power Sessions were never-ending church services!

I didn't vibe too well with some of those sessions, but they were pretty hyped. A lot of kids surrendered to Jesus, and I just fought the whole experience. To be honest, I just couldn't reconcile an all-loving, all-present, and all-powerful God with that of my life experience.

It was the last day, and there was one more Power Session to get through. I was determined to make it through untouched. We sat with our groups, but somehow there was a girl next to me from another group who looked like she visited from Gotham City. She had on thick eyeliner, a black top with a picture of a skull, jeans that went over her shoes and had chains hanging on them, and a studded belt.

As this Power Session went on, Harvey Carey, a pastor from either Detroit or Chicago, gave the message. It was a pretty dope message. I definitely resonated with what he said. The Nicky Cruz foundation did a dramatic presentation, and I liked that too. And then Anthony Evans led worship. Overall, the experience was pretty good. I still fought the emotions, and then it was time for what was called an "altar call." Hundreds of kids ran up from their seats and went down to the stage and just cried. That Gotham girl next to me started to cry, and if you have ever seen a girl with thick eyeliner cry before, then you can understand why I was "praying" to God to compel her to leave my presence and join all the other crazies at the stage. And she did! *Whew.* Yeah, I know. I was a jerk.

I was determined to stay where I was, and I wasn't going to give in to the emotions of the place. But then, I started to feel so heavy. I can't quite explain it well here, but I definitely felt something come over me like it was an invitation to take off the heavy backpack I was wearing my entire life and to lay it at the foot of the cross. After a brief wrestling moment with God, I couldn't hold back anymore. I cried and ran up front with the rest of them folks.

Gosh, I didn't know entirely what was going on, but I just couldn't take life anymore the way it was. When I was at the front of the stage, Harvey Carey called out, "You!" I looked up for a moment and noticed he was looking at me. I moved my lips and said quietly, "Me?"

Naw, I know you aren't talking to me. You don't know me. I just bowed my head a bit and tried not to make contact with him. But he called it out again, and I looked up and pointed a finger at myself.

He said, "Yeah, you."

Oh boy. Here we go.

He said, "You, young man, are going to be a pastor one day."

Ha! Listen, enough with that nonsense. I had other plans with my life. I argued with God in my head and let him know that I was taking things one step at a time. Wasn't running up to the stage to surrender my life to Jesus enough? And now, I'm going to sacrifice my dreams of being a firefighter or a SWAT officer? Come on now. I protested the whole thing.

Thankfully, Harvey Carey carried on and ended our time together that night with a message for all of us who surrendered our lives to Jesus. He urged us to do whatever was necessary to share this newfound faith with others and to use our gifts and talents to spread the good news of Jesus with everyone. I thought about that for a minute and told myself that I could do that.

The conference wrapped up, and we went home. Did things get better overnight? Not everything, but I did feel somewhat different. I talked with my youth pastor and told him I wanted to get out of the school I was in and to try a private Christian school where it could help me get a different grip on life. The problem was that private school was too expensive.

Within just a few weeks, he told me about this brand-new scholarship program that was being offered where they were going to select ten kids to go to one of three private schools in the area on a full four-year ride for high school. He urged me to apply and see what happened. What did I have to lose? I thought about it but hesitated a bit because no one was going to take a kid like me with the past I have.

I applied and went through most of the ordeal. Now it was the waiting period. During this waiting period, I remembered the challenge from Harvey to spread the good news. But how was I going to do that? Then it dawned on me. I had a plan.

I messaged my friend from school to meet me early the next morning at a paint store called Serve-U. The next morning came. He met me there, we went in, and we picked up two cans of spray paint. We stuffed these cans of spray paint in our backpacks and walked to school.

I waited for the perfect opportunity to implement my mission. The opportunity came when it was time for math class. I hated math class, so it was the ideal timing. I raised my hand to head to the bathroom. When permission was given, I took the can of spray paint and put it down my pants so no one could see. I went to the bathroom, took out the spray paint, and tagged the entire walls of the bathroom with "Jesus.'" Now everyone would know the name of Jesus who came into this bathroom.

Then, I realized that I probably shouldn't have done that. I felt guilty, my heart raced, and I began to sweat. You see, my middle school brain didn't really think ahead and process whether or not this plan was a good plan. Like a dumb criminal I was, I threw the can of spray paint in the trash and buried it with a couple of pieces of paper towels. No one would find out it was me.

I headed back to math class, and within moments, one of the school police officers came into the classroom with the vice principal. They went from desk to desk, and then I looked up to see them staring down at me. I guess I had the phrase "It was me" written across my forehead. They asked me to stand up and they brought me into the hallway. After a brief exchange of words, the officer read me my rights, handcuffed me, and escorted me down a few flights of stairs as the bell rang in time for classroom changes. Everyone saw what was going on.

I was brought to the local precinct, fingerprinted and booked, and then handcuffed to a metal bench. You can pretty much guess the next few weeks of events as I got grounded for months, had to appear before a judge, and deal with the shame that came with it all. Thankfully, the judge who was assigned to me gave me the option of either juvenile detention or community service hours plus full participation in church. I took the latter option.

In the midst of all this, I received notice from the scholarship foundation that I was initially going to be selected as one of the ten recipients, but not anymore. In light of my foolish actions, I was rejected, and rightly so.

When that news came, on top of everything else, I spent countless nights crying out to the Lord for help. I deserved all the crap that would come my way, but it drove me to my knees. I felt very hopeless and had no other option but to kneel before the Lord and cry out to Him. I pleaded with the Lord to forgive me, to please not let my foolish decisions map out a life of failure and despair. It dawned on me that I really did screw up, and I messed up that one opportunity at a life that would be so radically different than the one mapped out for me preconversion.

During those few weeks and months, I really couldn't see a future of hope. I felt so shameful and wondered if my "conversion" experience was even real. It was a really dark time of my life. I was suspended from school for quite a long time, couldn't see any friends, and couldn't watch anything on TV except stupid episodes of *Frasier* with my grandparents. Ugh.

This went on for a bit, and then I got a call. It was a call from the president of the scholarship foundation, wanting me to appear before the committee to give an account for my actions. I wasn't sure why I had to do that. Hadn't I gone through enough of the consequences already? Well, I didn't have much of a say in the matter and went to this scheduled meeting later that week.

I got to the room and stood before a handful of people. I felt even more shame and couldn't even look at any of them in the eyes.

The president of the foundation asked me, "What were you thinking, young man?" He then went on to say, "And even if you were given a second chance for consideration here, which you are not, why would we?"

I remember standing quietly for a moment with tears streaming down my face. I looked up and said to him, "Sir, you are right. If there was even a miracle of being considered now, it would be a pure act of grace, which I don't deserve."

The president, Paul, walked up to me, lifted my chin higher, stared at me in my eyes, was quiet for what seemed like eons, and then said, "I agree."

He hugged me, handed me an envelope, shook my hand, and said, "Don't screw this second chance up, and keep your eyes on Jesus, and get ready because you start classes soon."

I couldn't believe it! I didn't deserve any of this. I was shocked. I cried and wondered at how a perfect, holy God could lavish such grace on a screwup like me.

You see, Hannah didn't do anything to be unable to have a baby, and she wanted one. Me? I did everything to warrant the silence of God and the punishments I reaped, but God is so gracious and kind to lift us out of the valley experiences, whether or not the cause of those valley experiences lay on us.

We're all going to hit those "Hannah" moments where we cry out of desperation to God to hear us and to deliver us. I want to urge you to take those seasons and to be persistent in approaching God with the heaviness that's on your soul. Don't give up. God sees you.

You may struggle during those seasons of sadness and desperation with God's love for you. Yet Paul, who wrote a lot of the New Testament, writes this: "And may you have the power to understand, as all God's people should, how wide, how long, how high, and how deep his love is" (Ephesians 3:18). His love for you is too great for even Paul to put into our language. He sees you, He hears you, He knows you.

CHAPTER 6

Father of the Demon-Possessed Boy (Belief and Unbelief)

The older I get and the longer I serve in pastoral ministry, I hear more and more of the classmates I had during college deconstructing entirely away from their faith. I say "entirely" because I do think there is an element of deconstruction that's healthy, but when I hear many people say that they no longer believe in God when they used to, I wonder if it's deconversion instead of deconstruction.

I'll elaborate more on what I mean, but I'll say this: in most of the "cases" of hearing about people who deconstruct their Christian faith, there is almost always a journey of pain, loneliness, and sadness. Not always, but a lot more than we might be willing to admit. Before I engage this topic of deconstruction as it relates to depression, I want to immediately start off this chapter by looking at a story found in the ninth chapter of Mark's gospel. It's the story of the father of the demon-possessed boy.

There is a situation going on in which it got the crowds arguing with some of the teachers of the law. When Jesus appeared on the scene, the crowd saw him and ran into his presence. Jesus asked what was going on, and one of the men spoke up in response.

He tells Jesus that he has brought his son to him so that Jesus could heal him. The little boy is possessed by an evil spirit, and this spirit has prevented him from talking. It even throws the little boy to the ground in a violent fit. The little boy would grind his teeth and he would begin to foam at the mouth.

The dad asked Jesus's disciples to heal his little boy, but they couldn't. Jesus then accuses the people of having such little faith and demands that the little boy be brought to him.

When the dad brought the boy to Jesus, the evil spirit saw Jesus and threw the little boy into a violent convulsion as it forced the boy to foam at the mouth.

Jesus asked how long this had been going on.

The dad said it had been going on since he was just a little boy. The dad even said that the spirit would often throw the boy into water or fire, trying to kill him. He then proceeded to say, "If you're able to, help us."

Of course, Jesus said, "What do you mean by that?" Of course, Jesus is able to! Anything is possible if a person believes.

It was at that very moment that the father cried out, "I do believe, but help me overcome my unbelief!"

As the crowd got bigger and bigger, Jesus rebuked the evil spirit inside of the boy and commanded the spirit to come out of the boy and to never enter him again!

The spirit then screamed, threw the boy into another violent convulsion, and left him. When this took place, the boy appeared to be dead, and the people even began to say to one another that the boy was dead. But Jesus took the boy by the hand and helped the boy to his feet.

After this entire incident, when Jesus was now alone with the disciples, the disciples asked Jesus why they couldn't cast out the evil spirit. Jesus answered, "This kind can be cast out only by prayer."

Every parent is deeply protective of their children, or at least should be. When you see your child going through something so traumatic in life and there doesn't seem to be anything you can do tangibly, you start to feel a level of despair. No parent wants to feel helpless when it comes to their child. It breaks their heart. It grieves their spirit. It torments their soul.

And if you're a parent who's been following Jesus for a long time and then you have a child who 'falls off the deep' end and everything you do and say just doesn't seem to be helping your child the least bit, you cry out to Jesus and you say, "Help my child, if you can!"

We all know, deep down in the crevices of our soul, that Jesus can do anything. But we wrestle a little bit between believing this to be true and then struggling to believe that this is true at the same time. The father of the little boy cries out, "I believe; help my unbelief!"

One can only imagine the household of the little boy. Imagine that you are doing some housework, cooking dinner, or folding the laundry, and then you hear a loud crash, and you immediately know that your little boy has been thrown violently to the ground, or the fire, or the walls as a result of an evil spirit in him that you cannot do anything about. That is traumatic. It's an experience that's enough to shake you to the core, no pun intended.

I can only imagine the experiences of many parents who walk alongside their kids who go through experiences where they feel absolutely helpless. I've met a number of families who've watched their child go through the devastating effects of drug use. Their kids get addicted to drugs, and the drugs completely change everything there is about them. They become the polar opposite of who they used to be, and the mom or dad will cry out, "What happened to my little boy or girl?"

And often, in these experiences, the marriage comes under a huge amount of stress, and the experience greatly shatters the dynamics of not only the immediate family but also the extended family. While some experiences and journeys have a miraculous happy ending, a lot do not, as sometimes the grown child/emerging adult becomes homeless or overdoses. These are sad situations.

Traumatic experiences can really do a number on your faith. You so want to believe in the Jesus of the Bible, but you've been through so much that you are struggling a bit. You approach Jesus and say, "I really want to believe, but…"

So many people have gone through traumatic experiences in life, and they enter into a journey that begins with the struggle of believing everything they've ever been taught about Jesus. And in this journey, they experience a wide range of emotions from hurt, sadness, anger, bitterness, confusion, and a loss of wonder.

I mentioned earlier that deconstruction does have some really good things about the process, but if you're not careful, it can also direct you down a path that maybe you didn't intend to go down originally.

I'm not an expert on house projects. I just never grew up with anyone who could teach me how to remodel or fix things. Thankfully, there's YouTube and this new phenomenon of YouTube dads who teach us orphans how to do projects we never were taught.

I've bought a few houses over the course of the last decade and counting, and there is almost always a project that needs to be done that requires tearing down the old in order to build something new.

When I was in North Carolina for a few years, we had a pretty big deck in the backyard, but it was in rough shape. I never built a deck in my entire life, but I also was sort of broke. I was a youth pastor and we're usually the lowest ones on the totem pole in terms of pay. Enough said about that.

The deck needed to be done. Thankfully, the foundation was perfectly fine. It was just the deck boards and all the railings that needed to be torn down and rebuilt. I was really good at tearing down. The only annoying part was having to manually cut down the gazillion rusty nails that were ingrained into the foundational wood. Gosh, this took days.

Once that was done, we laid down the boards and used deck screws to do so. Then it was time to build the railings, which was surprisingly a lot easier than I anticipated. Then I stained it. Did it look like a professional did it? Nope, but it looked a thousand times better than before. I was proud of myself. But it took a lot of work, energy, and time.

When it comes to deconstruction, I imagine it is a lot like rebuilding my backyard deck. It needed to be done, it's painful at times, it's annoying at times, people critique the journey at times, and it's a journey to figure out the good stuff you'll use to rebuild it.

We're all constantly building a "faith home," and the hope is that this faith home has the foundation of Jesus and all the essentials of the Christian faith. Over time, you build upon the foundation using the "material" of your experiences.

Your experiences will vary from one another, but these experiences include camps and conferences you went to, denominations you've been a part of, college and graduate school communities you were engaged with, podcasts and books you've digested, pastors and religious leaders you've been influenced by (for better or worse), conversations that shaped how you perceive God and the Bible, news and social media outlets that influenced your perception of the church and Christians, and so much more.

Some of these experiences are good and some are not, yet they all contribute to the building of your "faith home." Maybe your siding is the experience of a negative Christian camp experience. Maybe the paint colors are the experience of your denominational experience. Maybe the flooring is the experience of a podcast in which you've listened to dozens upon dozens of episodes. Maybe the roofing is the experiences of how you saw the church respond to social issues over the years. Again, some of these experiences are great, while some are not so great, but they are all there in your house.

And then, one day, you felt like something was off about your "faith home." You weren't sure exactly what, but you entered into a journey to find out. You start to tear up the carpet because you don't like it at all. You scrape off the paint because it's the color of a denominational experience that gave you a picture of Jesus that doesn't resonate with the Jesus of the Bible. You take down that old paneling on a wall in a certain room that symbolizes an experience in a church where you were spiritually abused.

I hope I'm making sense here. I think it's actually a good thing to assess your "faith home" from time to time because not everything should be there. Some of the things in your "faith home" are there simply because you accepted it as gospel truth as a little child and never really took the chance to question the spiritual legitimacy of it.

I meet people all the time that go on this journey but there are two things I encourage them to think about. First, don't just tear everything apart and immediately throw it in the dumpster. Some of these things may still be really good, but it's tempting to throw it all out because you're angry, hurt, and deeply frustrated.

Second, in tearing down all those elements of your "faith home," be careful you don't tear down the foundation because the foundation is what you so desperately need, whether you realize it or not. The foundation is the Jesus you see throughout the pages of the Bible. The foundation is what will get you through those seasons of depression, despair, and loneliness. Without the foundation, you've got nothing.

But so many of my dear friends have torn down this foundation thinking that it'll lead to a more satisfying life. Maybe it will, but only for a short time. When you don't have the foundation of Jesus, you have no certainty, no hope, nothing to grasp onto when the storms come. And the storms will come again.

As I listen to the stories of countless individuals who are going through this journey, my prayer is that the journey will bring you to Jesus; not away from Him.

My prayer is that you can say, "Jesus, I so desperately want to have faith in you, but my negative experiences with the church are making that difficult." I think this is more than okay to do because there really are way too many negative church experiences that have done a significant amount of harm to people. I think Jesus would agree.

I know that when you go through this journey, it can be really, really difficult. Not only are you questioning the things you were taught and trying to figure out what belongs and what doesn't, but you're most likely getting attacks from other believers for being on this journey. They make you feel isolated and like you don't belong in the Christian community, and this makes things even worse.

If I could encourage you with something about this journey, let me say this: Bring someone trusted, wise, and seasoned with you on this journey. Don't walk it alone. You need to realize that the enemy is going to go full-on attack on you in this journey and is going to whisper a lot of things to you that'll be tempting to believe. He did it with Adam and Eve, and he will do it with you. Bring alongside someone who can help you process the journey, who will honor the confidence, and who will give you sound advice and counsel.

I think it would be a mistake to totally dismantle two thousand years of church history and tradition. While some of it is a product of its times and some of it is a bit off-base when you hold it in light of the Bible, there's so much of it that's enriching and that can strengthen your "faith home."

Not too long ago, I went through one of these journeys. I started serving as a pastor in the middle of the pandemic, and along came a year that was a bit difficult. Up until this point, I had never performed a funeral in my entire life, but I had to do quite a few for precious individuals who lost their lives to strokes, cancer, and COVID. I did so many of them that I didn't even need a handbook anymore to help me put a funeral together. I knew it by heart. Incredibly sad after only a year of performing funerals for the first time.

What made that particular year difficult was seeing your associate pastor and elder pass away unexpectedly. On top of this, your other associate pastor and elder moved away, and then you were left with quite the diminished staff from when you started. While all of that was going on, there's a pandemic that's happening and it's brutally attacking the church on multiple fronts. Ya'll know what I'm talking about.

Well, anyways, I began to question what the Lord was up to. I remember just sitting alone and asking God, "Why did you bring me here at this time for all of this to happen?" I really struggled to see any sign of hope in the near future. While asking those questions, I began to reflect on other aspects of my "faith home" that were starting to bother me. I think the pandemic, the increased globalization around us, the political and social tension, the elections, the negative press on the church, the fallout from Hillsong, the rapid decrease in church attendance, the abuse report on the church, the way the pandemic keeps changing people's ability to relate to one another, and the world events thrust a lot of people into a deconstruction journey.

Much has been revealed, and you're like, "Hold up. Something is a bit off between what I've blindly accepted, what's currently happening, and what I see in the Bible."

When I went through the journey, I started to ask questions like:

> "Why is *that* happening in the church?"
> "Why are Christians so callous toward *this* issue?"
> "Why do we preach one thing and constantly live out a totally different set of beliefs?"
> "Why is there complicity of the church in *this* area?"
> "Why does there seem to be so little of a difference between what happens in the church and outside the church?"

And I took full responsibility in any and all parts that involved me. You have to because none of us are perfect.

I then started to ask questions about my past experiences like:

> "Why did my denominational experience teach me that a certain group of people would burn in hell?"
> "Why was my wife and kids so mistreated on various occasions?"
> "Why did the church care so much about *this* world event but then turn a blind eye to *that* world event?"
> "Why did my pastor get ousted from the church with no severance pay to help support their small family?"
> "Why was there so much money allocated for church production but so little allocated for serving the poor?"

These are only a few of the questions I've asked, and it doesn't even begin to scratch the surface. I'll be honest with you. I began to grow bitter, and I began to allow several instances of church hurt to rewound me again. It brought me low, and I wondered if God cared. Of course, He does. I brought all this to Jesus and said, "I want to believe that you'll one day bring a better version of all this, but I'm struggling." I said, "Jesus, I see a whole lot of discrepancies between what we do as a church and what is outlined in your Word, and it's causing me to lose faith a little, so please help me."

I believed, but I needed God's help with my unbelief. I held those in tension, and I think many of our heroes of the faith did the same thing.

There's this story in the Bible that I always go back to when I wrestle with these emotions and thoughts. In Genesis 32, there's this man named Jacob. One night, he gets up and sends his family across the Jabbok River. When he does this, he is all alone.

When Jacob was alone, a man came along and began to wrestle with him, and this lasted until dawn. When the man saw that Jacob wasn't breaking, he touched Jacob's hip and wrenched it out of its socket. Ouch!

The man said to Jacob, "Let me go, for the dawn is breaking!"

Jacob refused to let him go until the man "blessed" him.

The man asked for Jacob's name, and Jacob told him. The man then tells Jacob that his name will no longer be Jacob, but he will be called Israel because he "fought with God and with men and have won."

When Jacob asked the man what his name was, the man said, "Why do you want to know my name?"

Then Jacob named that place Peniel, which means "Face of God." He did this because Jacob had seen God face-to-face and he did not die. As the sun rose, Jacob left Peniel, limping as a result of what happened to his hip.

Jacob wrestled with God, and so will you.

When I was a youth pastor, there was growing frustration that so many teens were "leaving the faith." And as I talked with parents, I would tell them that they are not necessarily leaving the faith. They are departing from their parents' faith and searching for a way to "own it." I would say, "If you've done all you can to present to them a faith that matches the Word of God, you've got nothing to worry about, but you need to allow them the time and space to take on this faith as their own."

So often, we hand off a "faith" that looks nothing like the Word of God, and we wonder why it doesn't last. Young people need to have the time and space to question things, to ponder and process all that they've been taught, and they need to know if their church is going to be a safe space to do so. Too many churches don't allow questioning, and this is a bad thing. If the Bible is true and Jesus is who He says He is (which I believe), then what do we have to worry about?

And it's not only young people that we need to allow this space for, but it's for everyone. There needs to be a space and time for dialogue, for debate, for conversations, for when this doesn't happen, people walk away.

I'll be completely honest with you. While it may seem so dark to walk through a journey of questioning, deconstructing the things that don't match the Word of God, and wrestling with God over various issues, there is a truth that a better faith will emerge. I believe that a faith that emerges from the intense heat of a small glowing ember is a faith that will sustain you through much of life. It's a faith that's been refined and continues to be refined. For me, it's easier to have faith when the flame is there, but my faith is reinforced and strengthened when I accept those moments when the flame isn't raging. Why? Because when the flame does come back, it comes back bigger and brighter than ever before.

My biggest prayer is that you don't give up. Maybe you feel like you've gone too far down that path and God wouldn't want you back anyway. Maybe it feels like you left home, and your mother or father said, "If you walk out that door, don't ever think about coming back."

Yet the door is always open to come back. God is so gracious and kind to us when we're on this journey.

Think about the story of the prodigal son. Often, when I preach about this story, I like to magnify the oldest brother's response because I feel we skip over this and we lose a major point in the story, but for our intents and purposes, I'm going to focus on the younger brother who almost threw away his life.

In Luke's gospel (chapter 15), there is a man who had two sons. One day, the younger son goes up to his dad and pretty much demands his share of the inheritance that's owed to him.

The father agrees and divides the inheritance between the two boys.

Shortly after this takes place, the little brother takes all of his stuff and hits the road. He moves away and it tells us that he wasted all his life on wild living. It doesn't take much of an imagination to know what this means.

But at a certain point, he ran out of money and a famine swept across the land. He became broke and started to starve. He got so hungry that he persuaded a local farmer to let him work for him, feeding the pigs. He got the job, and when he was feeding the pigs one day, he got so hungry that he started to entertain the idea of eating the stuff the pigs were eating. That's some intense desperation right there.

While entertaining this thought, he came to his senses. He realized that his father's hired servants had enough food to spare, and here he was on the verge of dying! He began to rehearse a conversation that he imagined he would have with his father when he got home, because he decided it was time to come home.

I always did this growing up. I sort of do it to this day. We get in trouble, realize how much we've really screwed things up, and we rehearse what we're going to say to the person we've offended. We do this out of worry and in hopes that what we say will somehow soften the blow.

He began his journey back home, and while he was still quite a distance away, his father saw him on the horizon. His father immediately ran to him. Back then, men didn't run because it would shame them. It was just a thing of their time.

But this father ran without question. His father was filled with love and compassion, and he embraced his son and kissed him.

While the boy began to spit out the words he'd so carefully rehearsed, the father interrupted him by ordering his servants to put on the biggest party ever because his son was once lost and is now found, was once blind but now can see!

While the party was going on, the oldest son was out there working in the field. He heard all the commotion and asked one of the servants what was going on. The servant told him, and the oldest son got really mad! He approached his father and said, "This son of yours." Whoa. What a way to disown your brother.

The older son started to complain that he'd been so obedient all these years and never even got a celebration, but when his delinquent brother came back home, he got thrown the biggest party imaginable.

There is so much we could unpack here with this story, but I don't want to lose the main point here. The point is this: You're never too far gone that God won't welcome you back home. Everyone goes on a unique journey at some point, and God the Father is always looking out at the horizon for your return.

I say this to the many people who are spiritually homeless right now and are craving to be back home with the Jesus they see in the Bible. Jesus is always looking to go after the one.

So where do we go from here? You find yourself in a very lonely space, trying to reconcile your belief in the Jesus of the Bible and the past negative experiences you've had or are having. You're struggling and you're not really in a good space right now. You feel worn out, burned out, empty, and you really don't know what's ahead for you.

You remember those days when the flame was big and bright, and this was a flame of tremendous passion for Jesus. You went on mission trips, served on awesome worship teams, talked about your faith with everyone, and then one day it all came crashing down. The fire died down, and all you're left with is a small glowing ember.

My friend, all hope is not lost. You are not alone. It feels like it because we've not allowed this sort of conversation and journey in many of our churches. It feels like it because people around you are calling you "faithless," but please be assured that so many people in the Bible have gone through what you're going through.

I'm praying for you, as the reader, to allow this journey to draw you to God; not away from Him. Earlier, I gave a suggestion to bring someone along with you. With that, pray. Pray the Psalms. Journal your thoughts. Be as honest as you possibly can.

The enemy wants you to be crushed and to feel so defeated. I once heard an admiral in the navy say, "Get up and make your bed." Sometimes, we don't know where or how to begin our day, but when we get up and make the bed, we are not accepting defeat. In the same way, when we get up, run to the Scriptures and don't let go. Cry out to God, "I'm not letting go until I can feel your touch on my soul, body, and spirit." You get up and you look at the devil in the face and say, "Not today, Satan."

You may think the enemy is strong, and this is true, but guess what? God is stronger. The author of 1 John 4:4 writes, "But you belong to God, my dear children. You have already won a victory over those people, because the Spirit who lives in you is greater than the spirit who lives in the world."

There is something here for us to learn. Don't take on the world yourself. Don't flirt with the things of the devil. The spirit of the world is very real and has every intention of deceiving you, destroying you, and defeating you. It is perfectly alright to say to God, "I am scared, and I am not sure what I'm doing or what's ahead, but I would like You to be with me and do a miracle for me." Yes, bring Jesus along because Jesus is stronger than the enemy. The enemy has already been defeated, and he is operating on borrowed time. He knows the clock is ticking, and all he's doing is taking anyone and everyone he can down with him.

One day, Jesus is going to come back and say, "Checkmate." He's already claimed victory when He died on the cross and then rose from the dead three days later. We anticipate His return.

For now, God's got something special for you, and I really mean that. I am not just saying that because I need words to fill the pages of this book. You are not a stat or a number. You are, according to Psalm 139, "wonderfully complex." God put in great consideration when He knitted you together in the womb.

And don't think for a moment that God doesn't grieve at the hurt and pain you experience in life. He does. But thank God, there is something better coming down the road.

CHAPTER 7

Naomi
(Facing Uncertainty)

Maybe this won't come as a surprise to you, but I worry a lot! Much to my dislike, I spend a lot of my time worrying, and sometimes it becomes debilitating. If anyone knows this, it's Victoria. She's the one who reassures me that everything will be okay. In those moments of worry, it can be days or weeks before I can get a grasp of my emotions.

Even when Victoria and I were in our dating years, I worried if I was good enough for her. I worried if she would leave me. When I married her, I would constantly ask her if she still loved me. I know it seems silly, but I had to work hard at overcoming this. I still struggle with this to this day, and my hope and prayer is that I'll keep building confidence.

I'm not really good at handling uncertainty. When I can't see what's ahead of me, I can get emotionally paralyzed. For me, when the future is uncertain, I begin to adopt a control mechanism, and this can be even more debilitating because it doesn't matter how much you try to control things. Life is out of our control more often than we like to admit. You can plan out the "perfect family day," and a truck can come plowing through the family car. That's a scary thought.

But to live each day in this constant fear can wear you down. It can bring you to the lowest point of your life, and it's no fun.

I don't often like watching reruns of movies unless they are exceptionally good. Not too long ago, I was watching *Dante's Peak* with my girls. I've watched this movie so many times and will still watch *Dante's Peak* over and over again. As I'm sitting there with my girls, I'm watching the movie like I've never watched it before. I am wondering what the ending is going to be. Isn't that ridiculous? One can say that if a movie can get you to feel that way every time you watch it, then it must be a good movie! At the same time, we all know how the movie is going to end because we've seen it before!

What's my point? I'm glad you asked. My point is that our life is like a film in the hands of God, and He already knows the end. We don't. We're watching our life unfold moment by moment, wondering what's going to happen next. Yet God is watching our life already knowing that there's a good ending because He's coming back! As hard as it is to live this out, it's just better to trust that God has a plan for you and me. There is no sense in putting that trust in us because we have absolutely no control in the grand scheme of things. And when we can't see what's ahead for us, what's the point in getting completely unraveled? There isn't, because all it does is push us into even more despair.

Again, this is easier said than done. In a sense, I'm writing to myself as well.

We all have that natural inclination to have control over the future. It's a natural tendency. Without control, we resort to fear and fear can drive us to become bitter, angry, and ultimately hopeless. It can bring us to some pretty low points in our lives. As I think about this, I think about the story of Naomi, which can be found in the book of Ruth, which is also in the Old Testament of the Bible.

This story takes place during the period when judges ruled Israel. The year was around 1300 BCE, which means that the story of Naomi took place 1,300 years before Jesus walked the earth, give or take. The book of Ruth is relatively short, with only four chapters, and I think it is worth just doing a brief survey of the entire book, sort of like I did with Esther.

We're told that a severe famine swept across the land. Remember, much of the Bible, if not all, takes place in an agricultural society, so a famine is absolutely devastating.

A man by the name of Elimelech ventured out from Bethlehem with his two sons and his wife, Naomi. They settled in the country of Moab. Today, that would be around the area of where Jordan is.

Once the family settled there, Elimelech died, and Naomi was left with her two sons. When a famine is present, women are left most vulnerable when there is no husband because the husband owns any land they have, and the woman owns no rights to the land. The only hope at this point in the story is with her two sons.

Her two sons, Mahlon and Kilion, found themselves wives. One son got married to Orpah. The other son got married to Ruth. We're not told much after that, except ten years passed and both sons died. This left Naomi in an even more grave situation. The cards were stacked against her. There was so much uncertainty ahead for her. Yes, she had her two daughters-in-law, but in that time and culture, this didn't matter much. All three were vulnerable and at risk of a bleak future.

One day, Naomi heard that the Lord had blessed His people in Judah (remember, this is where they originally moved to Moab from) by giving them good crops. They made the trek there. On the way, Naomi said to her two daughters-in-law that they should go back to their mothers' homes. She even prayed that the Lord would bless them for how kind they had been to Naomi and their husbands. Naomi wanted them to have a chance at a secured marriage. She kissed them goodbye, and they all broke down in tears.

Of course, they protested. Naomi fought back and explained to them that there was no future here with her. Naomi said, "Things are far more bitter for me than for you, because the Lord Himself has raised His fist against me."

Orpah agreed to go, but Ruth clung to Naomi and refused. She made this beautiful statement: "Wherever you go, I will go; wherever you live, I will live. Your people will be my people, and your God will be my God."

When Naomi realized that Ruth wasn't going to change her mind, she stopped arguing and just accepted it. They continued on the journey and arrived in Bethlehem. When they arrived, some of the townspeople realized it was Naomi and said, "Is it really you!?"

In response, Naomi urged them not to call her Naomi, but instead, Mara, because God had made her life really bitter and had caused her to suffer greatly. In her eyes, God had sent tragedy upon her.

Let's pause for a moment before going any further. In case you haven't picked up on it yet, Naomi was deeply wounded, and she had every right to feel this way. She lost her husband. She lost her two sons. She had no right to any land. There was a famine in the area. Women were not valued. Her future appeared bleak. Everything good had been taken from her.

One can only imagine what she was feeling. I am sure she had spent countless nights crying her heart out. I am sure she was deeply afraid of the days ahead of her. I am sure she felt crushed and hopeless.

Do you ever feel this way? Just when you think you have life figured out, it begins to pour in your life as you watch your entire life plan become dismantled one step at a time. Never in a million years did you think life would turn out this way. You had plans, and they don't seem to be working out. In seeing all this, you become miserable. People around you pick up on this, and you just sort of give up even trying anymore. You do the best you can with the resources that are left. You're basically just surviving at this point. You've lost interest in the things that used to excite you. You can barely crack a smile. You're tired all the time. You have no motivation to seek a way out of the mess.

Am I starting to ring a bell here? This is what Naomi was feeling.

While she was in Bethlehem, there was this wealthy and influential man there by the name of Boaz. Boaz was a relative of Naomi's late husband, Elimelech.

One day, Ruth told Naomi that she was going to go work the fields for anyone who was so kind as to allow her to do so. Naomi agreed with the plan and sent her off, and Ruth ended up working in the field owned by Boaz.

Boaz went out to the field and had some small talk with the harvesters, among whom was Ruth. When he laid eyes on Ruth, Boaz asked his foreman who she was. When the foreman told him who she was and that she had been the hardest worker there, Boaz approached Ruth and told her to stay on his land and not go to any other land. He even told her to help herself to some water when needed.

Ruth was overwhelmed with his kindness, and Boaz remembered Ruth's kindness toward her mother-in-law and assured her that the Lord would bless her for this.

Ruth had dinner with Boaz and then went back to the field to work more. Boaz ordered his men to drop some of the crops to make it easier for her to collect. This enabled Ruth to have quite an abundance, and Naomi was ecstatic.

Naomi was told what took place that day, and she told Ruth to just keep doing as Boaz directed.

The next day, Naomi instructed Ruth to make herself presentable to Boaz. At nighttime, she instructed Ruth to lie at the foot of Boaz's bed after uncovering his feet. She did exactly that. What does this mean? Well, it's basically a marriage proposal by the girl. They did not have sexual relations. It was a tradition in which women would lie at the end of the bed by the feet of a man in hopes that the man would marry them.

Boaz was a bit shocked because Ruth didn't do this to a younger man. Boaz realized that she was showing loyalty to the family in doing this and was greatly impressed. While he was impressed by this, he made it known that there was another man next in line to be the husband of Ruth should he accept it. Boaz wanted to do the right and proper thing first and see what happened. In order to protect Ruth, Boaz had Ruth left early enough in the morning so that no one would know what she did.

I am sure that Boaz was determined to settle things and to ensure that all proper steps were followed. That same day, Boaz met with the family redeemer. A family redeemer is someone who is next in line to marry a widow. In marrying the widow, the husband becomes a redeemer for them. How so? Because widows were at risk of a bleak future. They weren't protected. If they could find another husband, their at-risk future could be redeemed into a much brighter future. This is where the idea of a family redeemer comes in.

Boaz had a chat with the family redeemer, and after talking about a few stipulations regarding land purchase, Boaz made it known that if the family redeemer wanted to buy the land, then he must also marry Ruth. For whatever reason, the family redeemer didn't want to marry Ruth even though he wanted the land.

When that was settled, Boaz gladly took Ruth and married her! What a wonderful turn of events! As you'll find out in a second, this was also great news for Naomi.

As time passed, Boaz and Ruth ended up having a baby, and she gave birth to a little boy. Naomi took care of this baby as if it were her own. A neighbor said, "Now at last Naomi has a son again!"

This baby boy was named Obed. Obed became the father of Jesse, and Jesse became the father of David, who would one day become king. When you trace the course of family lineage from there all the way through the next 1,300 years, guess who you end up having? Jesus!

So this story is a beautiful micro picture of how Naomi and Ruth's situations were redeemed, and it's also a beautiful macro picture of how God's promise to send Jesus, the ultimate "family" Redeemer, couldn't be thwarted by a bleak chapter that we opened up the book of Ruth with. What would have happened had Ruth never had that little boy? How would the story have continued for the ultimate salvation of mankind with the possible break in the lineage in which Jesus was promised by God to have come from?

Goodness! Nothing can thwart the plans of God. And you want to know something? God is able to turn a bleak picture into a picture of hope. Way back in the beginning of the Bible when we read about the story of Abraham, God promised that Jesus would ultimately descend from his offspring.

Look at this: Abraham is the father of Isaac. Isaac becomes the father of Jacob. Jacob becomes the father of Judah. Judah becomes the father of Perez. You keep tracing that until you get to Nahshon, who becomes the father of Salmon, and Salmon becomes the father of Boaz.

So God orchestrates two big things here. He not only redeems Naomi and Ruth's situation that sort of looked bleak at first, but he protects the lineage of His promised Son, Jesus, at the same time by using the two of them. God is in control of the big picture and the small picture.

So often, we can't see that. We're watching the movie for the first time. In the pits of our grave situations, we're often wondering what God is up to. We're wondering what possible good can come out of our situations. And even when we feel that our lives have gotten way out of our control, we can rest assured that it's within the sovereign hands of God. Nothing takes Him by surprise.

How does this all work? I'm not God, so I couldn't tell you. I'm not going to sit here and pretend I have good enough answers for why God is allowing you to go through the things you're going through.

I'll tell you this, though: as much as foster care sucked and was just a terrible experience, I've had the pleasure of seeing my in-laws take in kids to foster and to adopt. Victoria told me a few times that they did this when they heard my story about being in foster care. I think that's pretty cool. That's a good thing that came out of something awful.

You see, we just don't always know the connection between things that we go through and how that impacts the lives of those around us. While there is much uncertainty at times, God is forging an ultimate certainty that we will one day see.

Did Naomi ever imagine that she would be holding the grandfather of King David? No, she did not. We know that by how she made those comments of despair shortly after the death of her husband and two sons.

March of 2020 came, and it completely scrambled the lives of every single individual on the face of this earth. All of a sudden, uncertainty was everywhere. For the first couple of weeks, there were a host of emotions ranging from anger, to "We've just got to get through two weeks to flatten the curve," to a bit of confusion and so on.

A couple of weeks turned into months and months turned into years, and then the devastating effects of the entire pandemic started to bubble to the surface. Kids were falling behind in schools, attendance in churches took a sharp decline, depression was at an all-time high, attacks on one another were rampant, the political atmosphere was nuts, people's personalities started to change, financial situations got bleak even with those stimulus checks, and the world felt the impact in ways we've not seen before.

In a very real sense, though it's been several years since the start of the pandemic, we'll be dealing with the effects of it all for quite some time. But one thing I've noticed that was a glaring issue was that people's joy was sucked out of them. Part of this is because of the weariness of it all, and part of this is from people's understanding that no matter the plans they put in place in life, it can all disappear in an instant.

If you turned on the news, which is such a bad idea at times, you're saying to yourself, "Here we go again." You're wondering if we'll be in another war soon, if a financial collapse is imminent, if the country is going to split, if the religious landscape of America is going to ever see the line going up, if the marriage is going to last, if gun violence is ever going to go away, and so forth.

The pandemic was brutal, and just when things have started to recover or open up again, you feel that something is way off, but you aren't exactly sure where to put the finger on. People changed. You changed. There seems to be very little interest in the things there used to be an interest in. You're worn out, tired, frustrated, upset that the legacy that was built prior all came tumbling down, and you're just unsure of what is ahead.

When the pandemic started, I was serving as a youth pastor in North Carolina. Up until the news that churches would need to shut down for two weeks, we had a really strong youth ministry. I was already there for three years at this point. We would meet on Wednesday nights for supper club, on Friday nights for a Hornet's game or laser tag, and on Sunday nights for a good ole' fashioned youth gathering with food, wild games, a lesson, and swimming at the lake. We went on mission trips often, and the environment of this youth ministry was pure gold. It was great! I loved it.

When we had to shut everything down for two weeks, we did things on Zoom, which definitely wasn't the same thing. And then another two weeks was added and then another two weeks. Even outside of what was shut down, we couldn't see each other because we had to social distance. As the weeks went by, I saw the youth ministry crumble before my eyes, and it absolutely broke my heart. It took a lot of work to build it up.

For a while, I was a bit angry. And then there was this level of uncertainty. Schools were shut down, which meant we needed to keep the kids home and watch them struggle to do online school, and it just wasn't working out. We struggled to balance this out and still work. We didn't have family where we were.

So Victoria and I decided to head back to New England where we grew up. What were we going to do up there, I was not sure. We decided to put the house on the market, and by September, we were living with her parents without any sense of direction. I started to apply at different churches, and there just weren't many openings because many churches closed their doors, and many of their financial situations were slashed due to the pandemic, so they couldn't take on a youth pastor. I did broaden my horizon and decided to see if pastoring was within the realms of possibilities.

But for a guy to just up and move without any sense of direction and without any sense of certainty was really difficult for me.

I spent about three months interviewing, and they were among the longest three months ever. When November came, I received notice that a big church in Connecticut had extended an offer for me to come on as their campus pastor. Personally, I was relieved that an answer was provided. But it was new territory to not only pastor, but to do this in a state I've never lived in before. Victoria and I prayed on it and decided to take the leap of faith and go. We would start in January of 2021.

But before we could start, there was the rest of November and December to get through. I worked briefly for UPS, which I really loved. Delivering all those Christmas packages in the cold weather of New England really wasn't that bad. I enjoyed it. This lasted for about a month until Covid hit me at the very end of November.

I wish I could say that it was mild, but getting that original Covid strain hit me hard. For most of December, I spent battling through in isolation and then in social distancing afterward. For a good two weeks, I couldn't hug my wife or kids, and that was hard. On top of all this, this had to be done through the holiday seasons and it was quite depressing.

Thankfully, I could be somewhat in the clear for Christmas Day, but I was severely exhausted still, and I had lost a ton of weight due to the sickness. Christmas day came and then the next day, we packed a U-Haul to move to Connecticut because I needed to start my role as a campus pastor on January 1st.

Whew. That was an intense, crazy period.

For most of that journey from March of 2020 through November 2020, I just didn't know what the future looked like. But God did all along.

To be honest, there were moments when I struggled to process my way through it. So much change in such a short time was difficult. Of course, this affected my ability to be the best husband and dad I could be. Again, I am grateful that they were so patient with me and that they loved me through it all.

Though it's a bit of a cliché, we're better off to let go and let God.

I find that when I go through seasons that impair my ability to see beyond ten feet in front of me, it's helpful to do the following:

First, take some time to reflect back on when God has come through. The God that came through back then is still the same God right now. While we may not know what the future holds, we can be sure that our world is in the hands of a God who is the same yesterday, today, and forever.

A good way to do this is to get into the habit of journaling, so when you go through seasons like the one Hannah went through, you can open up the journal and be reminded that not all is lost.

Second, surround yourself with other believers so that their faith can strengthen you. Christianity is a faith that's communal, and it's important that we don't try to venture through life alone. For me, there are a number of individuals I talk to for strength.

There's this story in the book of Exodus (chapter 17) where Moses struggled to keep his hands up with the staff in it. While he lifted his staff in the air, the Israelites had the advantage in battle. But when his arms grew tired and he lowered the staff, the enemy had the advantage. So Aaron, Moses's brother, and a dude by the name of Hur, helped Moses when he grew weary and tired. They would help lift his hands up in the air when he needed the strength.

When we go through those difficult seasons of uncertainty, sometimes we just need an Aaron and a Hur to help become our strength. We need people around us to encourage us, to strengthen us, and to reinforce our faith.

Third, let God fight your battle for you. Countless times in the Bible do we see God commanding others to allow Him to do for them what they can't do alone.

There is a verse in the book of Isaiah that I believe speaks to this. It says, "Listen to Me, descendants of Jacob, all you who remain in Israel. I have cared for you since you were born. Yes, I carried you before you were born. I will be your God throughout your lifetime."

Take that verse and put it somewhere that you'll see it every day. This is the same God Who wants to carry you through this season. Allow Him.

There are so many people who are exhausted, and my prayer is that the Church will become a place of refuge, where people can have their souls touched.

Psalm 42:4–5 says, "My heart is breaking as I remember how it used to be: I walked among the crowds of worshipers, leading a great procession to the house of God, singing for joy and giving thanks amid the sound of a great celebration. Why am I discouraged? Why is my heart so sad? I will put my hope in God! I will praise him again—my savior and my God!"

CHAPTER 8

Jeremiah (Remaining Faithful)

Why don't we just be honest and put all our cards on the table here? It is one of the most difficult things to remain faithful to follow Jesus wholeheartedly when you are going through a lot in life. It's difficult to follow Jesus when there's an obvious cost to doing so.

Of course, for me, I've gone through seasons in ministry when I really didn't want to trek forward anymore. There have been seasons when I felt so unqualified to do what I'm doing, and there have been seasons where I've felt like a total failure at what I was doing. I'll be the first to admit here that I've questioned my calling into ministry a few times before.

If you think every Sunday has been a great Sunday, it's a mistaken thought. There have been Sundays when I didn't want to get up and do what I was called to do because I just woke up feeling totally down. Sometimes I couldn't pinpoint the reason, and sometimes it's one of those Sundays that fall right in the middle of a very low season of ministry.

With the exception of one Sunday in 2023, I've pretty much just mustered up the strength to do what I was called to do and move on. Some of this has been through my own strength (which will only carry you so long), and many of those Sundays, I've had to ask God for a double dose of His strength.

EMBERS OF HOPE

The one Sunday I struggled on was the first Sunday of 2023. After a dark, intense December, I really did try to start off the new year on a good note because that's what we all try to do. I even drafted a New Year's mini message for the congregation. I was somewhat ready until I realized I was not. I got up front and right when I started to give this New Year's mini message, I got three words out and froze. Words just couldn't come out of me. I felt paralyzed. A thousand things were running through my mind, and I started to tear up and I literally just walked off stage, signaling to my associate pastor that he needed to take over. Just say something; anything.

It was a rough morning, and I felt so embarrassed that it even happened. It was like all the pressure from the past couple of years just came to the surface, and when this happened, I realized just how weak I was. I was humbled. Here I was spending all these years ministering to others and neglecting being ministered to.

A few people know about what happened that Sunday, and I am so thankful for the grace and patience that people had with me. Even though I am a pastor, I am also human, and I struggle with the same things that others do.

I know that not everyone reading this book would consider themselves in ministry in the traditional sense of the word, but perhaps you've gone through seasons as a follower of Jesus, and you didn't want to continue doing that anymore because the luster of your first days as a follower of Jesus wore off. Perhaps following Jesus cost you some friends, a little bit of popularity, and you felt like saying to God, "What am I even doing anymore?" Look at what the disciples did to Jesus right before He was to be handed over to the authorities.

Listen, we're going to get honest in this chapter. It's not that we haven't been thus far on this journey, but we're going to get down to the nitty-gritty of what it means to have faith when our soul is coming under attack.

For so long and in far too many Christian circles, we've adopted this idea that following God will pay dividends on our happiness, health, and wealth. It's not all doom and gloom for most who follow Jesus, but we need to be honest in saying that following Jesus doesn't guarantee that everything will be rainbows and unicorns. If our anchor in following Jesus is the temperature of our emotions and the products of our environment, we're in big trouble.

At the same time, when we anchor our souls to what Jesus *does* promise, we'll be able to take on what life throws at us. I believe that Jesus can help us not become unraveled in the battles of our minds.

In the Gospel of Matthew, Jesus says, "Come to me, all of you who are weary and carry heavy burdens, and I will give you rest. Take my yoke upon you. Let me teach you, because I am humble and gentle at heart, and you will find rest for your souls. For my yoke is easy to bear, and the burden I give you is light" (Matthew 11:28–30).

In a very real sense, there is a cost to following Jesus, but Jesus is able to sustain us, to carry us, to be the strength we so desperately need. For me, when I take the time to write out the costs of following Jesus and being in ministry, a few of the things that immediately come to mind are this idea that I feel so unqualified to serve God and that I have to battle so many things in my mind constantly, which makes it extra difficult to find joy in ministry at times.

I think that one of the tools the enemy uses against you in your walk with Jesus is to sell you lies. If the enemy can get in your head, he feels he's won. He wants to sow seeds of doubt in your mind. He wants you to think that God's abandoned you. He wants you to feel that God has given up on you. He wants to remind you of your past. He wants to give you all the reasons why you're not the right person for this. He wants you to feel that this whole Christianity is a farce. He wants you to feel that it's okay to step down for a bit in following Jesus, since you deserve a little break. He wants you to feel that the Word of God is outdated and it's perfectly okay to tweak it a bit to suit the kind of life that would be easier for you to live. I could go on and on, but this is what the enemy does.

Note: stepping down from ministry to get a little break to rest or because it's a danger to you or your family is not the same as stepping down from following Jesus. Just wanted to throw that out there.

And when the enemy promises that the grass is greener on the other side, you cross over and guess what? The grass is dead.

I will never claim that following Jesus is easy or that life will get easy for you once you do. Just take a brief survey of all the New Testament characters who followed Jesus and you'll find out.

Take Paul, who wrote much of the New Testament, for example. Look at what he writes:

> Are they servants of Christ? I know I sound like a madman, but I have served Him far more! I have worked harder, been put in prison more often, been whipped times without number, and faced death again and again.

He goes on to say,

> Five different times the Jewish leaders gave me thirty-nine lashes. Three times I was beaten with rods. Once I was stoned. Three times I was shipwrecked. Once I spent a whole night and a day adrift at sea.

And just when you think the list can't get longer, he adds,

> I have traveled on many long journeys. I have faced danger from rivers and from robbers. I have faced danger from my own people, the Jews, as well as from the Gentiles. I have faced danger in the cities, in the deserts, and on the seas. And I have faced danger from men who claim to be believers but are not. I have worked hard and long, enduring many sleepless nights. I have been hungry and thirsty and have often gone without food. I have shivered in the cold, without enough clothing to keep me warm.

He then ends by saying, "Then, besides all this, I have the daily burden of my concern for all the churches" (2 Corinthians 11:23–28).

Man, imagine this guy giving a praise update at one of the church's staff meetings.

But he's brutally honest. For Paul, yes, it is so worth the things he's gone through, but it isn't easy!

I don't want to paint a bleak picture of what it means to follow Jesus here, because it's not at all bleak. What's bleak is trying to live life without any hope in navigating it, and we do that when we handle things our own way. What I am trying to do here though is this: following Jesus is so worth the momentary "crap" in life we will experience in comparison to the eternity of unshakeable joy we will have.

Look at what Paul again says in 2 Corinthians 4:17–18:

> For our present troubles are small and won't last very long. Yet they produce for us a glory that vastly outweighs them and will last forever! So we don't look at the troubles we can see now; rather, we fix our gaze on things that cannot be seen. For the things we see now will soon be gone, but the things we cannot see will last forever.

When I read this passage, I am reminded that there are better days to come. For me, this doesn't mean to count all my current days as rubbish; no, it means that you and I can do this. We can stay on mission and remain faithful because these short days we live don't compare to what's to come.

But I get it though. These short days we live in seem so darn long and can be extremely difficult. But can you imagine just how much longer these days are when we have nothing to look forward to on the other side of the grave?

Perhaps you've gotten to the point in life where you feel you've already gone too far down the road of giving up. You've been out of the game of following Jesus for far too long that all hope is lost. Friend, all hope isn't lost.

Often, when I'm driving somewhere far away or to a place that's new, I get lost. I'm just not good with directions. Even with a GPS, I still manage to get lost. And when I get lost, my GPS will allow me the ability to get back on track and to recalibrate the map. That is an option for all of us.

You've had one of those bad days where the battle in your mind was so intense? Let's bring it to God and say, "I need your help."

I hate "battle of the mind" days. They are so discouraging. They are so heavy. They make me feel a bit debilitated. They make me lose focus. They make me feel that the days prior, even the so-called success days, were wasted. They make me feel entirely unsure of how to recalibrate the way forward. And for me, and possibly for you, the annoying and frustrating thing is that there'll be more of these days; more of these speed bumps and detour signs of life. One day, there won't be.

In this chapter, I want to talk about what it means to be faithful to following Jesus when you've been tempted to walk away from it all and to do this, I'm walking us through a bit of Jeremiah's life. This is a bit different from what we talked about in a previous chapter about deconstruction. This chapter isn't about the struggle to believe; it's about the struggle to persevere and endure when your soul is groaning.

Jeremiah is a major prophet in the Bible. Prophets were basically mouthpieces for God to the people. God would tell a prophet what to say to the people, and the prophet would do exactly that. Well, sometimes there's a fight between the prophet and God, such as in the case with Jonah where God told him he had to go and preach to this wicked city of Nineveh and Jonah responded by literally running away.

See, I told you. Even the big shots of the Bible and our Bible heroes struggled a bit. So will you. So will I.

Jeremiah's life and story covers a pretty wide span of chapters in the Old Testament, so we will really be dealing with a general "high view" of his story and zeroing in on a couple of specific instances in his life where I believe there's something for us to grasp onto.

Jeremiah did his prophetic work between 626 BC and 587 BC. He received the calling from God in 627 BC when he was just a young man. While there is much debate as to how old he was when God called him, there is a consensus that he was anywhere between the ages of fifteen and twenty. Some scholars even put his age younger. We do know that he was still dependent on his parents.

Right when we open up the book of Jeremiah, we read that God started to give messages to Jeremiah beginning in the thirteenth year of the reign of Josiah all the way until the eleventh year of the reign of Zedekiah, who were kings by the way. That is five kings total, and all these kings ruled the Kingdom of Judah. This would put Jeremiah's "ministry" close to fifty years! That's a long time.

In the first chapter of Jeremiah, it tells us that the people of Jerusalem were taken away as captives in the month of August of that eleventh year of the reign of King Zedekiah. We'll come back to that detail in a bit. I talked briefly about this in the chapter on Elijah, but it's worth noting that it's been close to three hundred years prior to when the nation of Israel split into South and North when we open up the book of Jeremiah and read about his calling as a prophet.

God called Jeremiah to speak on His behalf to a nation that had gone pretty much off the deep end, but He did this by saying, "I knew you before I formed you in your mother's womb. Before you were born I set you apart and appointed you as my prophet to the nations" (1:5).

This is an awesome passage because it tells us that God had Jeremiah in His care and in His hands even before Jeremiah was born! Sometimes, we struggle to think that our lives are worth anything, but the truth is that God knew you and had you in mind before the day you were born.

By natural default, Jeremiah responded to God's call here with the excuse that he was far too young for this!

Have you ever given God an excuse? Perhaps it's your upbringing that makes you think that you're not the right person. Perhaps you think your lack of education disqualifies you from doing great things for God. Perhaps it's what you've been told that you've sort of just accepted as truth about yourself. Perhaps you think you're too screwed up to be successful in a ministry area. Perhaps you're looking at what's ahead and thinking to yourself, "I already feel like my head is going under water to even take this on."

I am sure a million thoughts were going through Jeremiah's head right then. This was not an easy task that God had asked of

Jeremiah, and Jeremiah knew this. I am sure there was also a level of fear in him.

When Jeremiah gave his excuse, God said, "Don't say, 'I'm too young,' for you must go wherever I send you and say whatever I tell you. And don't be afraid of the people, for I will be with you and will protect you. I, the Lord, have spoken!"

In those moments that you feel so weak, remember that God is with you. It's not just the weakness of our exterior world, but it's also the weaknesses we experience inside of us that He's with us too. God is the God of your mind; not just everything else. If God can fight the battle of what people can see, He can certainly fight the battle of what people cannot see.

This is important because we'll feel alone in this battle. I commend the church for coming alongside people in helping them in the battle of overcoming finances or their marriage troubles, but it's the unseen battle of the mind that people feel the most lonely in. God is with you in those battles. When no one else understands, God does.

Here is a note on this though: there's this popular idea that's going around that says that God will not give you more than you can handle. I will say this: Yes, He will. He most certainly will. He's done it to many people in the past, He's doing it to many people today, and He will continue to do it to many people tomorrow.

So why does God give us more than we can handle? Because these battles we go through were never meant for us to fight them alone. When we fight them alone, we become defeated. The strength we have isn't adequate enough, but the strength that God gives you is sufficient to carry you.

The bulk of Jeremiah's life was speaking to a people that wouldn't listen to him. Jeremiah constantly rebuked the people of Israel and warned them that judgment would come if they didn't stop worshiping false gods! I mean, the people had really rejected God and had gone so far off the track, and God, in His right and just judgment, warned them of what was to come.

So what was coming? The people of Israel were surrounded by enemies all the time, and one of these enemies was the Babylonian empire. Jeremiah touches briefly on this in Jeremiah chapter 20. He basically told them that they would lose the war against Babylon and they might as well just surrender.

And sure enough, Babylon came in 587 BC and totally collapsed Israel's society. It was King Nebuchadnezzar who did this, and if you'll remember some of the Bible story, you'll remember that it was Shadrach, Meshach, and Abednego who were thrown into the fiery furnace by Nebuchadnezzar for not bowing down and worshiping a golden statue of a false god. If you are not familiar with this story, take a few moments and look it up. It's a pretty incredible story!

Jeremiah warned Israel that this would happen and he came head-to-head with a guy named Pashur. Pashur was the man in charge of the temple and he got hold of one of Jeremiah's messages and decided that he didn't like his message one bit. Pashur then threw Jeremiah into the stocks after arresting and whipping him.

The stocks were wooden frames with holes to lock in the head, arms, and legs. It was a painful, excruciating experience, and Jeremiah had been a prophet for about twenty-two years at this point. Being put in a wooden stock was a method used to "break" rebellious spirits.

Jeremiah spent barely a day in the stocks before he was released. What did he do next? He delivered the same message to Pashur as the day before! He remained faithful even after all he had been through. He would not quit and give up.

From our human perspective, Jeremiah had every reason to give up. By today's standards, he was not really successful in ministry. No one listened to him, and everyone wanted him dead. If Jeremiah were around today, he wouldn't make it one day on the staff of any church. He would not garner any viral videos on social media and would have the least popular podcast ever.

We might think, "He is so much more bold and courageous than I can ever hope to be." But did Jeremiah not exchange some words with God about his struggles? That's where we get to next.

In Jeremiah chapter 20:7, we read about a very low point in Jeremiah's life. He seems to resonate with how we can feel often. This section reads like a very private conversation between God and himself. We get to peek into Jeremiah's public ministry and the deep struggles he had privately. These are two separate things.

Imagine that Jeremiah had one of his days trying to be faithful to God, and this was what everyone saw. Then he got home and was brutally honest with God about how he was really doing.

I know exactly how this feels. For many reasons, you must "hold yourself together" in public ministry but then decompress privately. I'm not always good at this. My poor wife often deals with this with me, and I am so thankful for her patience. For me, and most likely for you, I need an outlet to process the difficulties of the day. This outlet will look different for everyone. For me, sometimes it's writing and journaling, sometimes it's taking alone time for a walk with music, and sometimes it's finding someone trustworthy to confide in.

Do you feel like this sometimes? You're trying to "hold it" together but release the side of yourself no one sees when you get home? People think everything is okay, but it's not. You're in pain, emotionally distraught, tired, worn out, angry, feeling a bit hopeless, and you bring all this to God privately and say, "I really want to continue to remain faithful to you but I'm struggling here."

And why do we separate the public moments from the private moments? For various reasons: fear of what happens when others see the "true" side of us, to protect something bigger than ourselves, because no one will understand, and many more. While the characters of the Bible were brutally honest publicly, they found private moments and spaces to wrestle with God alone. We need both public spaces to be honest with each other and private spaces to wrestle deeper with God.

Look at these words from the prophet: "O Lord, you misled me, and I allowed myself to be misled. You are stronger than I am, and you overpowered me. Now I am mocked every day; everyone laughs at me. When I speak, the words burst out. 'Violence and destruction!' I shout." After really getting going, he says, "Yet I curse the day I was born! May no one celebrate the day of my birth…Oh, that I had died in my mother's womb, that her body had been my grave!

Why was I ever born? My entire life has been filled with trouble, sorrow, and shame" (20:14, 17–18).

Yet Jeremiah continued to serve God and be faithful. God is so kind as to allow us to bring our raw emotions to Him. I do believe that God works with us and through us in those moments.

If you're married, you might be familiar with moments of tension with your spouse. Those moments, believe it or not, are necessary for the two of you to grow deeper together. When those moments are not allowed, you grow away from each other. In those moments, you hear each other out, you speak the things on your heart, and you resolve to come together with a new way forward. You do this because you love each other. You communicate with each other. You're honest with each other.

When I went to college to study youth ministry, I also decided to take every single class focused on missions as my electives. I did the same thing for every class focused on juvenile justice. But when I took those missions classes, I became intrigued by the many men and women missionaries who lived extremely difficult lives yet remained faithful to the task that God had assigned to them. In fact, I couldn't put down the books that talked about their lives. I was strengthened, encouraged, and challenged to know that the strength of the gospel really can and does sustain us through difficult trials we may go through.

One of the missionaries I studied, but was also familiar with from former years, was Adoniram Judson, who was a missionary in Burma, which is present-day Myanmar. This guy, as well as his family, suffered so much, yet was so persistent in making sure that the people he was reaching knew about Jesus someday.

His father was a pastor, yet when he went off to college, Brown University, he became a skeptic of the gospel. Then his friend tragically died, and this bothered him so much. He ended up petitioning to go to seminary, and it was there that he became a believer in the person and work of Jesus. While Adoniram was in seminary, his heart and passion burned for missions. This is what he wanted to do.

So he spent the next few years in preparation for this venture ahead. While doing so, he married a wonderful woman by the name of Ann Hasseltine. When they were married, they were ordained as missionaries and set sail for India with two other individuals. This made them the first Americans to venture into the unreached population of the world with the gospel.

Behind the scenes was this intense work to bring awareness back to the states about missions and to raise funds for this. This didn't come without complications. While all this was happening, Adoniram Judson began to learn the language of the people, which is the Burmese language. His goal here was to not only fit in with the culture but to also eventually translate a Bible into the language of the native people.

The Judsons were no strangers to suffering. In fact, three of their children sadly passed away, and Ann became really sick, which forced her to return back to the United States to seek treatment for two years. She then returned to Burma.

In 1824, an intense war broke out in the country of Burma, and this led to Adoniram's imprisonment. He spent nineteen months in prison overseen by guards who had been convicted of murder. While in prison, Adoniram struggled immensely, and Ann did everything she could to keep her husband from dying in there. She even sewed his translation of the Burmese Bible on a pillow and was able to give that to him.

He was eventually released, but within months, Ann died of smallpox. Ann was able to translate the book of Jonah and Daniel into the Burmese language. Shortly after her death, at thirty-six years old, their little two-year-old girl died six months later.

Adoniram Judson fell into a dark grief period, which led him to retreat for forty days into the jungle, where he even dug his own grave. He did return, and people were shocked that he survived this period. Judson was resolved to not give up. His passion to reach the Burmese people for Jesus would keep pulling him from the darkest moments of his life.

As a missionary, though he had eight kids in total, three of them died as infants. As mentioned above, his first wife died of smallpox. His second wife died of an illness en route to seek treatment. His third wife, Emily Chubbuck, died of tuberculosis at the age of thirty-seven, though it was a few years after Adoniram Judson died of a serious lung disease.

When Adoniram passed away, he had completed the entire Burmese Bible translation, left behind twenty-six churches, and over five thousand converts. Before he arrived in Burma in 1813, there were none.

Of course, this is a really brief sketch of this great man of God, but it is worth noting his faithfulness despite having gone through so much in life. He lost his wives, lost three of his eight children, suffered greatly while in prison, received no accolades on the field, and fell into seasons of intense depression. He also suffered from sicknesses, diseases, extreme temperatures, and seasons of despair.

When his wife, Ann, died of fever, Adoniram sat by her grave and wrote, "God to me is the great unknown; I believe in him, but I cannot find him." He was in a very dark place in life, and this is totally understandable.

Here was a man of faith who, though we may not be able to relate to every circumstance of his life, we can receive encouragement and permission to be human. He also gives us hope that success in following Jesus doesn't mean escaping the realities of depression, loneliness, and sadness. Success is resolving to be faithful in the midst of it all. And we're able to do that when Jesus becomes the source of our hope.

One of the things I wish we would do better at in our churches today is to define accurately what success as a Christian, church, or ministry means. We're so ingrained to think that it means bigger buildings, better programs, more people, epic content, and attractive legacies.

Yet when I pore through the pages of our Bible, I am wondering if most of our Bible heroes would fail to reach the standard of today's definition of success by the church. What if success is all about being faithful when the times are difficult? What if we release some of the undue pressures we put on ourselves and each other?

CHAPTER 9

Jonah
(When Bitterness Festers)

Jonah is one of my favorite small, dramatic books of the Bible to read, to study, and to glean some incredible insights from. The reason why I am choosing him here is because I remember reading him say, "Just kill me now, Lord! I'd rather be dead than alive if what I predicted will not happen."

Of course, I'll be giving a lot of context to that statement, but as I was going through the pages of this small book of four chapters, Jonah was really bitter and miserable. As I thought about this, I am reminded that going through seasons of depression, when we only have a small glowing ember, can be incredibly difficult, and if we're not careful, can lead us to bitterness toward not only God Himself, but the people around us. We can become so miserable, and God doesn't want this for us.

For me, I remember getting this way from time to time, and it can be quite catastrophic to those around us. This will be a hard chapter to write because none of us want to be told to stop throwing a temper tantrum in aisle 8, but there's something really important for us here. Having gone through this, I want to share with you my heart and some of the things I've learned during those seasons. I'm not saying it's easy. I'm saying that there is a difficult decision we must make when bitterness starts to take root in our hearts. There's an intentionality to all of this. First, let's set the story.

Jonah was a prophet who lived during the reign of King Jeroboam II, who ruled in Israel (the Northern Kingdom) in the first half of the 700s BC.

One day, God spoke to Jonah and told him to go and deliver a specific message to the big city of Nineveh. The message was that God would judge this city because of how bad they were. Nineveh today is a city in present-day northern Iraq.

Now how did Jonah respond to this? Immediately, he got up and went in the opposite direction. He ran away. He was trying to get away from God and God's mission for him. He was not having it. This was not something that he was going to do, and nothing was going to change his mind. Nineveh was a wicked city. In Jonah's mind, he knew exactly where this was going to go if he did as God asked of him.

If he did what God commanded him to do, that city would listen, would repent, and would turn from their evil ways. He didn't want this. He didn't think they deserved God's judgment to be terminated by doing all this. If we slow down a bit in reading this story, you'll begin to see remarkable similarities between the story of Jonah and the story of the Prodigal Son. In the Prodigal Son parable in the New Testament, who was it that got so angry at his father for forgiving his younger brother after everything he did to the family? The elder brother! I'll share more of this story shortly but keep that in mind.

Jonah found a ship leaving for Tarshish. While there is debate as to exactly where Tarshish would be today (some think it is southwest Spain), what we do know is that it was quite some distance from where he currently was at this point in the story. Joppa is where the port for the ship was. That is present-day Tel Aviv, Israel. He wasn't just going down the street. He was looking to get away as far as possible at that moment. It is estimated that he was attempting a 2,500-mile journey in the opposite direction! That's serious commitment to run away from God!

This tells you how much he did not want to do what God commanded him.

So he got on the ship. God sent a storm. It was a powerful storm. The storm was so powerful that it threatened to break the ship in half. Fearing for their lives, the sailors on the ship called out to their gods and started to throw any cargo overboard to lighten the load.

While this was happening, Jonah was asleep down below. The captain yelled at him in disbelief and demanded that Jonah cry out to his god.

When things were not getting better, the crew cast lots to determine who was at fault. The lots, of course, identified Jonah as the culprit.

When forced to identify himself, Jonah said that he was "a Hebrew and he worships the Lord, the God of heaven, who made the sea and the land."

The sailors were super afraid, especially when he told them that he was trying to run away from God. When asked what can be done, Jonah just told them to throw him into the ocean. Instead of doing that, they tried to row harder against the sea, but they were not successful.

They began to cry out to Jonah's God and plead with Him to not make them responsible for Jonah's actions, for God to spare them. At that point, the sailors picked Jonah up and threw him into the ocean. Immediately, the storm stopped. As a response to the storm stopping, the sailors made a sacrifice to Jonah's God and vowed to serve Him going forward.

While Jonah was unwillingly making his way to the bottom of the ocean, God arranged for a big fish to swallow Jonah, and Jonah remained inside this fish for three days and three nights. This is all in the first chapter of Jonah.

In the second chapter, we are privy to the details of his prayer to God while he was in the belly of this whale. Was it a whale or a big fish? Doesn't matter. No one wants to spend three days and three nights in the guts of either.

This prayer is pretty deep. In it, he recognizes the holiness of God and all that God has done for him. He vows to follow God and to do all that He says. Almost like a re-dedication moment. I don't know about you, but if I were in Jonah's situation, I would most certainly do the same thing! I mean, apart from a miracle here, you're sort of stuck and about to die!

After this prayer, God orders the fish to spit Jonah out onto the beach! Can you imagine? Jonah is just lying there on the beach and is covered in fish guts. Can you imagine the smell!? Gross.

Almost immediately, in chapter 3, God is offering another chance to Jonah to go to Nineveh and deliver the message that He has given him. Imagine God saying, "Shall we start this over again?" Of course, this time, Jonah obeys!

He takes the 550-mile journey and delivers this message to the people of Nineveh. And guess what? The people believed him and declared a fast to show their sorrow! When the king heard about this, he dressed himself in burlap and sat on a heap of ashes and made a decree to go through the entire land.

If you're wondering about the burlap stuff, basically it was a piece of clothing made from a black goat's hair. Often, mourners would wear this to signify their remorse and repentance. This was not a comfortable piece of clothing, which served as a reminder of the discomfort of repentance.

The king's decree called for everyone to turn from their wicked ways, and here is what the last verse of that third chapter says: "When God saw what they had done and how they had put a stop to their evil ways, he changed his mind and did not carry out the destruction he had threatened."

This is great news! But Jonah did not think so. In fact, Jonah burned with anger and knew that this was exactly what was going to happen. This is why he didn't want to do this in the first place.

We turn our attention to the fourth and final chapter of Jonah's story, and we see Jonah complaining. Notice what he says here:

"Didn't I say before I left home that you would do this, Lord? That is why I ran away to Tarshish! I knew that you are a merciful and compassionate God, slow to get angry and filled with unfailing love. You are eager to turn back from destroying people."

And then he makes the statement to God to just kill him now. Oof!

My goodness. The boldness that Jonah has here to say all that. But in reality, you and I think this in our hearts more often than we are willing to admit. We're really no different than Jonah. Just think of how steeped in anger Jonah was at God to get to the point where he would rather just have God kill him now. This is an intense feeling.

What I want to do here is recognize that he has some serious things to work through that, if he is not careful, can lead him down a very dark path. Why? Because bitterness, resentment, and anger can lead us on a very dark emotional journey. It is a cause of depression that's not talked about enough. I've actually experienced this before, but first, let's finish that last snippet of the story.

As Jonah is getting things off his chest, he finds a spot to just sit and watch Nineveh from afar. It obviously got super hot because the story tells us that God arranged for a big plant to grow in order to provide Jonah shade. Just as soon as Jonah was liking this shade, God arranged for a worm to eat through the stem of the plant, rendering the plant dead! God then arranged for a scorching east wind to blow on Jonah. Jonah began to grow faint and then said, "Death is certainly better than living like this!"

God asked Jonah if it was right for him to be angry that the plant died. In response, Jonah shouted, "Yes!"

In a quick rebuke, God got angry at Jonah for caring about the death of a plant more than the twelve thousand people living in spiritual darkness! Ouch!

The story ends in the same way as the "prodigal son" story does. We don't know how Jonah reacted to God's rebuke. We don't know Jonah's response, just like we don't know how the prodigal son's older brother responds to his father's wish for him to come in and celebrate his brother's return from wild living.

All we know is what he last said, which was, "Even angry enough to die!" Jonah was so upset that God forgave this wicked city.

Why? Because Jonah obviously had resentment toward Nineveh. He didn't think they deserved God's compassion, grace, and forgiveness. Jonah thought they didn't earn it, which was so contrary to how God operates to begin with.

God lavishes His love, His grace, His forgiveness, His kindness, His compassion on us because He wants to; not because we deserve it. We don't. This is what makes God's love for us so radical. His love is so radical in that He sent His one and only Son, Jesus, to die on the cross on our behalf so that we can have eternal life and life to the fullest.

I mentioned earlier that when we hold on to resentment and bitterness in the same way that Jonah does, it can lead us down a dark path. The good news is that we can work through this. Through therapy, excellent resources, and a community of compassionate friends, we can come out the other side as brighter people. There is amazing freedom when we release ourselves to forgive, to see the other offending party as people whom Jesus loves.

Let me say that last part again: to see the other offending party as people whom Jesus loves. The question for you really is this: Who is your Nineveh? Who is your younger, prodigal brother?

An article on Johns Hopkins Medicine (hopkinsmedicine.org) said this: "People who hang on to grudges, however, are more likely to experience severe depression and post-traumatic stress disorder, as well as other health conditions. But that doesn't mean that they can't train themselves to act in healthier ways."

As a pastor, I see tons of people who struggle with this, and it breaks my heart seeing the devastating toll it takes on an individual when they refuse to let go of resentment and bitterness. When we hold onto bitterness, did you know that we are, in a sense, playing God over another person's life? And at the same time, when we hold onto bitterness and resentment, we end up hurting ourselves more than the person we're attempting to hurt with our coldness? Interesting how that works. Holding onto a grudge for any reason never, ever works out in your favor.

In fact, in holding onto a grudge, you end up losing way more than you bargained for. The longer we hold onto resentment, the more we lose, such as all that energy that could be going toward something so much more positive in your life. As a result of lost energy, you miss out on any potential in your life because you're spending it all on harboring bitterness. This takes up space in our mind and demands all of our attention that can be focused elsewhere.

I've met people who've held onto bitterness for more than two or three decades, and this has led them to a life of absolute misery.

We see this played out in so many ways. We see a person resenting their ex. We see a person resenting someone who has lied to them. We see a person resenting a family member who did them wrong. We see a person resenting a boss who mistreated them. We see a person resenting a person who did something terrible to them years ago. We see a person resenting a specific race or people group. We see a person resenting someone who holds a different political view.

And all of this leads to misery, and misery can lead you to a depth of darkness you never knew existed. Oftentimes, we do this to ourselves.

"But," you protest, "you have no idea what this person has done to me." You are correct. I don't. But I can share with you how holding onto resentment in my personal life toward those who've harmed me has brought nothing but disaster. I can share with you that I've wasted so much of my life holding onto bitterness toward those who were unjust toward me. I can share with you the anger I held onto, the sadness that it brought me, the loneliness that sprouted, the negative thoughts that were produced. It literally held me in bondage, and then I felt stuck; unable to break into true freedom until I finally grasped onto the gospel and what it all means.

If we take a minute to really think about this, when we choose to hold onto bitterness and resentment, we are literally allowing ourselves to be controlled by another person. The delusion is that you think you're the one controlling them by withholding forgiveness. It's quite the opposite.

For years, I held onto resentment toward my father who was never there. He left before I was even born. I still don't even know my father, yet I allowed my father—a man who doesn't even know me—to be the center of my anger. For years, this anger took control of my life. I started to behave in unhealthy ways. I started to think unhealthy thoughts. I started to play the victim. And for what? For a man who is probably sleeping like a baby? For what? For a man who has moved on? Isn't it crazy when we think of it like that? Nothing was going to change. He wasn't going to pop into my life and start being "Dad." And who is to say that things wouldn't be worse if he did so?

I had to release my anger. I had to forgive. But forgiveness went deeper than just wanting to not be controlled by my anger. Forgiveness needed to be rooted in the gospel if we are to truly be alive and free.

It took years to figure this out. One day I was steeped in prayer, and the reality of my sin hit me hard. Who was I to think I was better than the people I resented? And what does it compare to the pain and hurt I've caused and continue to cause Jesus, who willingly died for me?

The level of offense I've caused Jesus doesn't even compare to the level of offense I believe the other person caused me.

When we start to play God in deciding who is worthy of our forgiveness or not, we're emphatically declaring that the gospel isn't for everyone. We're declaring that the love of God must be earned. We're also declaring that our offense toward God really isn't that big of a deal.

I had to get to the point where I could answer to Jesus when He asked, "Do you believe I died for your father? Do you believe I laid My life down for the people who did bad things to you?"

This was a hard pill to swallow. If a person turns their life around and comes to recognize Jesus as Lord, Savior, and King of their life, then that person is redeemed by Jesus. You might be tempted to say, "Yeah, but most bad people like the ones we resent won't end up surrendering their life to Jesus, so it doesn't really matter."

Here's the thing, though: it's not a matter of who we think is good or bad. We can always think we're a pretty decent person when we compare our lives with others. But when you compare your life with the standards of God, which we miss, then the reality sinks in. The tragedy is that most "good and decent" people will be spending eternity under God's judgment. The gospel puts us all in the same boat. There's one way to be redeemed. There's one person Whom we're all redeemed under, and that's Jesus. It's really that simple.

When we take all this and take some time to dwell on it, our posture toward those around us changes, including our enemies. I think that when most Christians read the phrase "love your enemy," we're somehow talking about a far-removed people group or potential type of person. No, the enemy is the one whom we hold resentment toward.

Does this mean it'll now be easy to do so once we grasp the nature of the gospel? Absolutely not. But we have a choice, and it's an intentional choice we must make. For the rest of our lives, we'll be put into positions where we need to choose to love and forgive or not. And when we make that difficult choice to love and forgive, we're being spiritually formed into the kinds of people that Jesus desires us to be.

When we look at the story of Jonah, he didn't think the Ninevites were worthy of God's compassion. What this means is that he believed he was. Why, though? Because he was a prophet? Who ended up winning in the story? The Ninevites. They found freedom. Who ended up losing in the story? Jonah, the prophet. He's the one who ended up in misery while the Ninevites were celebrating the goodness of God toward them.

Turn to the story of the prodigal son. It's found in Luke's gospel. The younger son demands a share of his inheritance. He is given it. What does he do? He goes out and lives like a wild man until one day his money is depleted. A famine comes over the land, and he finds himself longing to eat the slop the pigs would eat.

Then he comes to his senses. He begins to rehearse what he's going to say to his father after all that he's done because he's planning to return home. He begins to make the journey home and the story tells us that his father sees him on the horizon. His father has been looking for him; looking toward this day. While his son was still a long ways away, the father runs toward him.

Before the son could even begin speaking his rehearsed apology or excuse, the father demands a huge party of celebration thrown for him because his son was lost and is now found!

While the party is going on, the father's oldest son is out working the field and asks one of the servants what's going on. The servant tells him and this angers him so much! His father pleaded with him to come in and join but the older son refused.

Notice what the oldest son says: "All these years I've slaved for you and never once refused to do a single thing you told me to. And in all that time you never gave me even one young goat for a feast with my friends. Yet when this son of yours comes back after squandering your money on prostitutes, you celebrate by killing the fattened calf!"

The story leaves us with a cliffhanger very much like Jonah. We don't know if the eldest brother finally realizes the gospel or not. We don't know if he eventually ends up coming to the party. And I think the cliffhanger was intentional by Jesus. It's a message for us. What will we do? What will our posture be toward those whom we think don't deserve God's love?

In the prodigal son story, the eldest brother thinks that the father owes him due to his obedience. The father, obviously, represents God and the eldest brother represent religious people.

Why do I share all this? Because what we truly believe about the nature of the gospel is directly tied to our resentment, bitterness, and unforgiveness. When we grasp the gospel correctly, we can break free from the vicious cycle of darkness and depression that anger and resentment so often throws us into. There's a true freedom and healing that can take place.

Now let me be clear on something here: what I've shared is just a fraction of the pie when we correlate resentment and bitterness with depression. I believe it's a large fraction, but oftentimes, seeking additional help with our anger and resentment is a must. Why? Because sometimes there's so much to unpack depending on how long we've held in resentment. Sometimes we need help seeking healthy coping mechanisms when it comes to our emotions. Sometimes we need professional help because there are other factors involved when it comes to our resentment.

I am only merely sharing, as a pastor and as one who've experienced this, a certain perspective I've seen when it comes to the relationship between one's view of the gospel and one's view of the person that they must chose to forgive or not forgive.

I am merely sharing out of a burden that I've seen so many people's lives turn to devastation when they've chosen the path of bitterness. I've also seen so many lives transformed when people gain a maturity in their understanding that Jesus has died for the *whole* world. And since we are talking about characters in the Bible, the lens I am writing is a gospel lens.

Imagine if Jonah had grasped what God was trying to communicate to him. Imagine the bitterness and resentment, and all its effects, he could have avoided if he had merely seen Nineveh and its people as individuals for whom God wanted to rescue.

Imagine if I had grasped earlier in my life that the cross wasn't just for me; it was for my father and for all those people who did such terrible things growing up, should they accept it. Imagine all of us if we had striven toward this posture.

But what about the resentment that builds up in us that we're not quite sure comes from? You woke up on the wrong side of the bed; everything irritates you, and you just seem mad at the world, but you can't pinpoint why. What you can pinpoint is that you've been like this for days or weeks, and there doesn't seem to be any way to snap out of it.

The longer this goes on, the more that people around you are affected. The more that you are affected. It feels like this resentment of some sort started off as a seed (still not sure how it got planted there) and then it sprouted until one day it feels like a fully blooming ugly flower. This ugly flower is just a symptom of what's now going on in your heart, in your mind, and in your soul.

You were angry at work. You were angry at your spouse. You were angry at your kids. You were angry at church. You were just angry, and every little thing was a trigger to your anger. The people around you did nothing wrong to you, but you were angry. Whether it was a jaded kindness, passive aggressiveness, or the cold shoulder, you weren't vibing with anyone. You weren't even vibing with the dog or the perfect weather.

Then one day, you couldn't even figure out the point in life. You lost purpose in absolutely everything you did, including the things you once loved to do. As the days passed, you felt heavy, then sad, then self-pity, and then you suppressed it all. The people around you wondered what happened. Heck, you didn't even know what happened. It just did. You didn't want to be this way. You just didn't know how to get back your joy. You needed help getting it back, but you were also afraid of asking for help because someone may spread your story to another person or betray your confidence.

You may even have had a day here and there where something brought you a small jolt of happiness, but then it was gone like a vapor in the wind. What happened? You got even more down because that small jolt of happiness was just a tease. So where did all of this come from?

One thing I can say for sure is that this resentment that appeared to come from nowhere is the result of buildup. It's a result of unhealed past trauma of some sort. It's the result of suppressing anger on top of more anger. It's the result of unhealthy coping mechanisms when we're in an environment that triggers us.

In short, the "sudden" resentment, anger, irritation, frustration, and bitterness are the growing tip of an iceberg.

I know this to be true for me personally. I've gone through seasons just like this, and each day and week and month I let pass felt like a growing snowball that was bound to get out of control. This growing snowball would become packed with sadness, unhealthy thoughts, anger, and depression; and it would run over anyone that got close to me.

The good news with all this, though, is that we can get this all under control with a combination of things.

First, you have to bring this to Jesus. Seriously. You have got to be completely honest that this has gotten out of control, and you are hurting people around you as a result. You need to ask Jesus to breathe His healing breath down to the depths of your soul, because it's more than the symptoms you want treated. You want to unroot what's causing these symptoms of irritability, outbursts, impatience, loneliness, etc. If we don't get to the root of it, the snowball continues to get bigger and bigger.

Second, get help from a professional therapist. A therapist will journey with you to the root. They know what questions to ask. They know what tools will help. My recommendation? Find a therapist who is Christ-centered.

Third, find an accountability crew whom you can trust. You want someone who you can confide in, and you know will not betray your confidence. You also want someone who is going to say the necessary hard things that you *need* to hear. As tempting as it is, what you don't need is someone to put fuel on the self-pity party we tend to put on for ourselves. We don't need guests to that party. You need someone who can speak the truth to you as well as do it in a compassionate, kind way.

Fourth, you need to find a church that talks about this. What I mean by that is that the sermons, Bible study content, and community group framework need to go deeper than surface level. The mistake churches often make is preaching motivational TED Talks to make you feel good. Listen, the gospel is good news, but the process of getting well is hard work.

Listen to what a man named Paul wrote in his letter to an ancient church in Rome:

> So the trouble is not with the law, for it is spiritual and good. The trouble is with me, for I am all too human, a slave to sin. I don't really understand myself, for I want to do what is right, but I don't do it. Instead, I do what I hate. But if I know that what I am doing is wrong, this shows that I agree that the law is good. So I am not the one doing wrong; it is sin living in me that does it.
>
> And I know that nothing good lives in me, that is, in my sinful nature. I want to do what is right, but I can't. I want to do what is good, but I

> don't. I don't want to do what is wrong, but I do
> it anyway. (Romans 7:14–19)

Until Jesus takes us to our eternal home, we're at battle with our flesh. It's a spiritual warfare, and war is never easy.

You need the church to equip you for battle. You need a church to send you into the battlefield with the tools and methods for success. We are not preparing our people for battle today, unfortunately. We are not preparing our people today to venture through some of the most difficult things life throws at us. Much of our messages are only good for when life happens to be going good for you.

Because here's what I learned through some of these seasons of bitterness and resentment: most of it boiled down to my heart posture, my attitude, and what I chose to do with the season that I was in. Yes, life was so unfair at times, but life was always going to be that way this side of eternity. There was no sense in trying to escape the realities of life because it was impossible.

You really needed Jesus to get you through this. And you needed Jesus to do heart surgery on you as you got through this. For me, it wasn't always about getting through a difficult season, but rather, it was about discerning what the Lord was wanting to do with me in the midst of that season.

For Jonah, God wanted him to check his heart's posture toward the people he hated the most. Think about it: even though Jonah had massive success in his preaching to the Ninevites and getting them to turn their hearts away from evil, God didn't even recognize it. God was more concerned with his heart and the poison that was infecting it.

As I wrap up our time with Jonah, a few themes emerged from his story that I think are very applicable to us.

The first is that Jonah tried to run away from God. As I was thinking about this, I wondered how often we try to run away from our problems that may be causing us to stoop so low in life?

How often did we enter into a new year and promise a new me? How often did we change schools so that we could get a fresh start? How often did we change relationships because the last one was a really bad one? How often did we change our addresses for a fresh, new beginning in life? How often did we change churches in the hopes that this one would be the one that would make us happy?

Now I recognize there are times we must change locations and situations, especially if they are very unhealthy and causing us serious harm. But let's consider this: When we ran from one place to the next or one situation to the next, did it end up actually being better for you? What I found is that the root cause of our depression followed us no matter where we went unless we dealt with it properly. When we didn't deal with the root cause, we ended up bringing the same seed to the next location, relationship, and situation.

I also recognize that we're often scared to get to the root. We're scared of what we will find, but the good news is that God is waiting to embrace you. We've been so conditioned to thinking that God is vindictive and is a bully, but this is so far from the truth. He desires true freedom for you. God is the father in the prodigal son story where He is always looking out on the horizon for you to come back home.

Another theme that emerged from the story of Jonah is the fact that God had full control of things. If we noticed in the story, God appointed a storm to disrupt Jonah's travels, God appointed a plant to grow to provide shade for Jonah, God appointed a worm to eat the plant, God appointed a scorching wind to go in the direction of Jonah.

Your journey was not a mistake, and the things that happened on your journey did not take God by surprise. I am not saying that God appointed absolutely everything in your life, but everything in your life was within the scope of God's knowledge. I think we have a hard time believing this.

When we ventured through our misery, we often said things and did things that we never thought we would do or say. We were left horrified and then believed that God rinsed his hands clean of us and abandoned us. No, when God called you, he factored in all the stupidity we would be engaged in. This is really important for you to hear.

My advice for you is this: be aware of those moments that start to throw you off balance. Those moments when we began to bubble up with bitterness were trying to tell us something. It was trying to get our attention. Slow down and be aware of those moments and tend to those moments. Invite the Lord into those moments and say, "Okay, Lord, I am aware of what's happening, so let's tackle this together."

Be honest with yourself. Don't try to deny that there's something slightly off. Don't try to muscle your way through all this. Don't throw up your hands and say, "It is what it is." No, those moments, as messy as they can be, are sacred moments in which the Lord wants to do something incredible in your soul if you'll have Him.

CHAPTER 10

King David
(It Can Happen to Anyone)

It can happen to anyone.

It doesn't matter your status, the position you hold, the accomplishments you have, the great family you might come from, the degrees you hold, the awards you've accumulated, the past you have, the stellar reputation that people have of you, the titles you possess, the circle of people you're a part of, the money you bring in…

It can happen to anyone.

Read the following passage for me. It's a Psalm straight out of the Bible.

> Have mercy on me, Lord, for I am in distress.
> Tears blur my eyes.
> My body and soul are withering away.
> I am dying from grief; my years are shortened by sadness.
> Sin has drained my strength; I am wasting away from within.
> I am scorned by all my enemies and despised by my neighbors—
> Even my friends are afraid to come near me.

> When they see me in the street, they run the other way.
>
> I am ignored as if I were dead, as if I were a broken pot.
>
> I have heard many rumors about me, and I am surrounded by terror.
>
> My enemies conspire against me, plotting to take my life.

It can happen to anyone.

It can happen to King David, who wrote the Psalm above.

This is the king who, as a little boy, slew the giant, Goliath.

This was the little boy who was the great-grandson of Ruth and Boaz, whom we discovered in a previous chapter. This was the man through whom the lineage of Jesus would travel through. This was the man who was "God's anointed one." This was a man who was an exceptional musician. This was the man who was a mighty warrior.

This was the man who would be Israel's mighty and greatest king. This is the man who would father the wisest man who ever walked the face of this earth, Solomon. This was the man who would be known as a "man after God's own heart." This was the man who wrote a very large portion of the Psalms in our Bible.

Yet this is the very same man who experienced some of the deepest valley experiences that exist.

Yeah, it can happen to anyone.

Why do I say this? Because depression has no favoritism. It's actually a sobering reality, and for me, it makes me a bit nonjudgmental toward the person going through it. Not that we should be judgmental to begin with.

For some strange reason, we tend to think we're somehow immune to the effects of our emotions' darkest avenues. Of course, I thought this once. I mean, don't we tend to think this way when everything in life is going well? Out of sight, out of mind.

Then it hits us. We then become more aware of everyone else going through it. We become a bit saddened that we've sort of turned a blind eye to others going through it.

Whenever I open my phone and get news stories of a famous faith leader (or really, any leader) who does something we never imagined would be possible for them, I'm sobered. I'm, in a strange way, relieved. I think, *So they really are human like me.*

Because when we struggle with something so dark, we feel we're alone. We feel it only happens to people who are screw-ups, outcasts, dirty sinners, low people. And those people tend to be hidden because they've been pushed to the fringes of society. As a result, we're crying out in our souls, "Where's my people? Where are the ones who can understand me and what I'm going through?"

If I'm going to be real with you, the church becomes a place where this regularly takes place. Sundays are supposed to be our "emotional high," right? Christian circles are places where it's easy to see all this on full display. You look around and everyone seems to have it all together. You don't dare counter the culture. You don't want to "ruin the vibe" for others.

Yet here's what's interesting: it's all masked.

In a congregation of high-level lawyers, doctors, successful leaders, business owners, Instagram-perfect families, influencers, coaches…there is, behind a thick veil of imposter-like material, depression, anger, sadness, loneliness.

I would consider myself an empath. When I'm tuned into this gift, I can read people. I am very observant. This can be my biggest asset and biggest thorn in the flesh. I read body language. I read the eyes. I analyze language and tone. Why? Because there's almost always a story that no one's telling because they are afraid to tell it. They are afraid there is no room for their narrative, for their story. So they remain silent; hidden.

And what I find is that it's the people who are successful on the outside who hide it. "It can't happen to me, right?"

Yes, it can.

The ones who don't appear successful on the outside are more prone to showing it. And the successful ones know what happens to them, so they suppress all negative feelings to avoid the consequence of being real, honest, authentic, and open about their struggles.

I mean, at initial glance, who can blame them, right? The consequences are so devastating. You're avoided like the plague. No one wants you at their party. It's lonely as heck. No one understands. Help is a bit superficial.

When I was in middle school, my friends were not the popular ones. It wasn't by design. It was just the way it worked. When I did gain popularity in the later middle school years, I was pressured to let go of "those" friends.

My friends were part of the emo crowd. It was a bit of phase for me as well. A longer phase than I planned. I wore the big bell-bottom jeans with the chains, thick leather and studded bracelets, a studded belt, and yes, even black-painted fingernails.

I didn't quite listen to Metallica or Korn as much as they did. I settled for Linkin Park. And Simple Plan. Oh, and Evanescence. I felt they produced music that spoke how I was feeling on the inside.

But these friends went super deep. I still stuck with them, though. The more I got to hang out with them, the more similarities I found we had. Rough upbringing. Abusive home environments. Bullied to oblivion. Anger at the world. Coping issues. The whole nine yards.

I also found out that their world was lonely. On the outside was this emo toughness, yet they went home each night and cried. They rarely let that fact be known. No one who rides a skateboard for a living cries.

But they did. Some of them cut themselves. Some of them did drugs. Some of them drank until they passed out. Some of them intentionally did illegal things to get arrested. They felt they didn't have anything to lose. What was the point of life? No one cared. No one would miss them, they thought.

This was the crowd I ran with for a couple of years. And before that, I ran with a totally different crowd. It was the crowd that bullied the emo crowd.

This crowd fought a lot. There was a lot of exterior "toughness" to this crowd. In a group setting, they were seen as ones to be feared. They carried weapons on them. They did what others dared them to do despite the legal consequences. Some of them were part of gangs.

Some of them just grew up in tough neighborhoods, and this lifestyle was expected of them.

Yet here is what I found interesting: behind that veneer of toughness was brokenness. I remember going to one of their homes to hang out, and I saw my friend break down in tears when his mother yelled at him. When he saw that I saw, he said, "If you tell anyone about this, I'll kill you."

This was a person who had no problem bullying others and causing bodily harm to others. He acted out a lot in class too. People sort of feared him. Yet when you peel back the layers, he was lonely on the inside. He had issues at home where he felt abandoned and ignored. His father was never in the picture.

Doesn't matter who you are. It can happen to anyone.

I chose King David for this very reason. Of course, if we placed all his cards on the table, a good portion of his grief was brought on himself when he slept with the wife of a commander in his army and then had that commander intentionally killed. But, equally, a lot of his grief was brought on simply because life is unfair at times.

He went through a lot. Here was a man, though, who had every resource at his disposal to 'shield' him from grief of all sorts.

Think about it. How often do we try to shield ourselves from suffering and depression? We tend to think that if only we had enough, if only I was in a different situation or location, if only I had this or that, then could I be happy and avoid the pitfalls of depression. King David had just about everything, and he plunged to the depths of the valley. He was not immune.

One of my favorite things about King David and this Psalm that we read above is that he didn't lose hope. Despite how dark his circumstances were at times, he still had tremendous hope in God. Read the rest of this Psalm that he writes:

> But I am trusting you, O Lord, saying, "You are my God!"
> My future is in your hands. Rescue me from those who hunt me down relentlessly. Let your favor shine on your servant.

> In your unfailing love, rescue me.
> Don't let me be disgraced, O Lord, for I call out to you for help.
> Let the wicked be disgraced; let them lie silent in the grave.
> Silence their lying lips –
> Those proud and arrogant lips that accuse the godly.
> How great is the goodness you have stored up for those who fear you.
> You lavish it on those who come to you for protection, blessing them before the watching world.
> You hide them in the shelter of your presence, safe from those who conspire against them.
> You shelter them in your presence, far from accusing tongues.
> Praise the Lord, for he has shown me the wonders of his unfailing love.
> He kept me safe when my city was under attack.
> In panic, I cried out, "I am cut off from the Lord!"
> But you heard my cry for mercy and answered my call for help.
> Love the Lord, all you godly ones!
> For the Lord protects those who are loyal to him, but he harshly punishes the arrogant.
> So be strong and courageous, all you who put your hope in the Lord!

King David clung to the Lord and God invites that. Oftentimes, God becomes our everything when we're faced in a situation where God is our only thing. We realize that the world is a dark place to navigate without Him. There have been moments in my life where this rang so true.

I remember someone once told me that it took way too much faith to believe in a God. I responded that it took way too much faith to take on this world without belief in God. How does one just say, "It is what it is"? It's quite miserable to live with a framework like that. It's hopeless.

Yet when we seek God in the midst of our depression, what do we really have to lose by doing so? Blaise Pascal, a mathematician and philosopher, once said, "Let us weigh the gain and the loss in wagering that God is. Let us estimate these two chances. If you gain, you gain all; if you lose, you lose nothing. Wager, then, without hesitation that He is."

I can tell you with certainty that you have nothing to lose by seeking God in the midst of your troubles. I can equally tell you that nothing else we seek to remedy our afflictions works.

But you may be wondering, "Where is God?"

I can assure you that if you seek Him, you will find Him. There's this verse in the Bible that I really love. It's written by Jeremiah (remember him?). He wrote what God had said to him: "If you look for me wholeheartedly, you will find me. I will be found by you."

Isn't that amazing? Now, that's a promise. But God doesn't force Himself on you. He waits to be wanted, and when we find Him, the extraordinary happens.

Quite often, when we are journeying through that which is so painful, we rather, albeit stubbornly, handle things our own way. Which, by the way, never really works in our favor, does it?

With that said, the opposite is also true. God knocks on our door. And He is so gracious to keep on knocking. But when He does knock, it might be by way of us hitting rock bottom or us coming to our senses that our ways are just not working.

In the very last book of the Bible (Revelation), Jesus says, "Look! I stand at the door and knock. If you hear my voice and open the door, I will come in, and we will share a meal together as friends."

Notice the tone. Jesus desires to commune with you as friends. He is gentle. And I can tell you from experience that when someone is going through depression, a gentle spirit means the world.

For years, Jesus has been knocking on my door. I kept ignoring the knock. I wanted to handle things my own way, and when we do that, the tendency is that we become destructive. When we handle things our own way, we're also looking for ways to numb the pain. Numbing the pain actually only makes things worse, and the devil knows this.

He entices you with promises of allurement, He promises things that will cure you and bring relief, but it only throws you further down the pit. The devil is good at this. He always over-promises and always underdelivers on those promises. But God keeps his promises always.

There was a period in my life as a young boy when I would drink a lot. Drinking was a way to escape the pain.

When I was in middle school, I remember bringing a water bottle to science class filled with vodka. I was in so much pain emotionally. I am not sure what I was thinking that day, but I would drink from that water bottle throughout class little by little, and then someone said something to me. I'm not sure what he said, but it triggered me. I got up from my chair and went to confront this individual and was about to take a big swing at him.

Before I could throw hands at him, my science teacher ran to me, bear hugged me, and tackled me to the ground. Want to know what he whispered in my ear?

He said, "You're better than this."

I didn't believe I was, but in retrospect, that whisper was one of those knocks on my door from God. It was a knock that I eventually would open the door for.

I had a hard time believing I was better than this. What could God do with my mess? What could God possibly want with me? I was so emotionally unstable. I'd done terrible things. I felt broken beyond repair. I felt there was no future ahead for me.

But God knocked, and I answered. He came in and dined with me as a friend. Since then, God has been tender to my soul. Has it been an easy road? Nope. Has he been so gracious with me every time I backslid? Yup. I'm blown away at God's crazy grace.

Let's go back to King David.

In his darkest moments, King David knew no other way than to cling to God. Only God could rescue him from his predicament. Only God could pave a way forward for him. Only God could make sense of what he was going through.

King David was able to not lose hope, but how? As I look at his life, I can't help but think it's because God has been so good to him in those moments when he knew he really screwed up. A portion of King David's life I want to dive into is how do we navigate the emotions that come when we really screwed up in life?

I think it's a valid question because so many people are overwhelmed with dark thoughts when they've done something unimaginable. They are overwhelmed with a guilty conscience and think that they've really canceled out God's love for them.

Maybe this is you. Maybe you've gone through this. Let's take a look at King David's situation and then let's see what it means for you and I when we're going through moments of guilt.

The story can be found in 2 Samuel 11. I'll paraphrase here.

One day, King David stayed back from a battle when he should have gone out.

By doing so, King David was walking on his roof when he noticed a beautiful woman bathing on top of her roof. He immediately sent someone to find out who she was. When word got back to him, he called for someone to bring her to him to his place. When she got to his place, he slept with her. Being a king during that time, we must understand that she really didn't have a choice in whether or not to come.

After the affair (she was married), she became pregnant and told King David this news.

What did he do? Well, he summoned Bathsheba's husband, Uriah. When Uriah came to meet with him, King David carried on a casual conversation asking how the war was going. He then released Uriah from the war and told him to go home and relax. But Uriah didn't go home.

When King David found out, he asked why he didn't go home to relax. Uriah didn't feel comfortable just staying home relaxing, and sleeping with his wife while his men that he commanded were at war!

King David tried again and insisted that Uriah go home and sleep with his wife and "relax."

Notice here that King David was trying to cover up what he did. If he could get Uriah to sleep with his wife, he could easily deceive others in thinking that it was Uriah who got his wife pregnant. But when this effort failed twice, King David did the unfathomable.

He sent a letter instructing Uriah to go to the front lines of war. He instructed the men to pull back when the fighting got intense and leave Uriah to be killed. This was exactly what happened.

Yes, you heard all that correctly. David slept with another man's wife, tried to cover it up, had a casual conversation with the husband as if nothing happened, and then had him arranged in war to be intentionally killed. Oh, and one can argue that he used his position of power to his own advantage by sleeping with a vulnerable woman.

At the end of 2 Samuel 11, Bathsheba received the news that her husband was "killed in battle," and she grieved over this. The text tells us that when her period of mourning was over, King David sent for Bathsheba to come and be one of his wives. She then gave birth to the baby. The chapter ends by telling us that God was displeased with what King David had done.

Okay, hang in there with me. There's a bit more to the story. In the next chapter (12), a prophet (Nathan) confronted King David. Nathan told a parable that got King David furious at the plotline. King David was so furious at the plot, he said, "As surely as the Lord lives, any man who would do such a thing deserves to die!"

Well, Nathan said, "You are that man!"

King David must have been a deer in headlights. Nathan then said, "This is what the Lord says: Because of what you have done, I will cause your own household to rebel against you. I will give your wives to another man before your very eyes, and he will go to bed with them in public view. You did it secretly, but I will make this happen to you openly in the sight of all Israel."

Whew. Goodness.

There's more.

King David then confessed his guilt. He said, "I have sinned against the Lord."

Nathan replied, "Yes, but the Lord has forgiven you, and you won't die for this sin. Nevertheless, because you have shown utter contempt for the word of the Lord by doing this, your child will die."

Brutal.

After this encounter had taken place, King David went home. A deadly illness struck the child, and David begged God to spare the child. He went without food all day and night and lay on the bare ground. On the seventh day, the child died.

You can be sure that this wrecked King David.

Now, you might be wondering a lot of things right now. What does this all have to do with what I'm going through? How is any of this story good news for what I'm going through? If God punished King David that way, wouldn't I be next? You might be thinking, "Yeah, well, King David deserved everything that was coming his way."

You might have other thoughts, but whatever those thoughts may be, allow me to share with you a few takeaways.

First, when we are being spiritually corrected by God, this means that God loves you enough to correct you. You must not lose sight of that. The scary part is when we 'get away' with our sin and move on as if nothing happened and still have that guilty conscience on us.

In Hebrews 12:6, it says, "For the Lord disciplines those he loves, and he punishes each one he accepts as his child."

We need to take into account that God takes sin seriously. Why? Because sin is cosmic treason. God is a holy and righteous God, and sin is a violation of a holy and righteous standard.

I became so aware of this when I got into major trouble in eighth grade. My youth pastor sat me down when I was going through a time of intense depression following what I did. I tried to respond by saying, "I made a mistake." He said, "No, you made a decision."

That decision was to do the opposite of what I knew would please God. The conversation was what I needed to hear; not what I wanted to hear. God was interested in restoring me, but I needed to come to grips with all of this. I then realized that God loved me enough to discipline, but the discipline was followed by restoration.

For many of us, we never get to the point of restoration, and this leads us to being bitter and resentful and deeper in our depression. This brings me to my next takeaway.

It's that we've been conditioned to view God and how he handles and views us through the lens of our unhealthy experiences.

For a long time, I viewed God through the lens of an absent earthly father. And then I continued to view God through the lens of many present abusive fathers in the foster care system. I allowed my experiences to dictate who God was instead of allowing the Scriptures to reveal to me who God is.

It doesn't stop at discipline. There's restoration. Just like Jesus restored Peter after being denied by Peter three times, God desires to restore us.

The good news is that all the mess we've gotten ourselves into will one day be redeemed. We will one day look forward to the absence of tears, pain, depression, and suffering.

When we read the story of King David and the loss of his baby, did you notice what he says in 2 Samuel 12:23? David says, "But why should I fast when he is dead? Can I bring him back again? I will go to him one day, but he cannot return to me."

I believe this is a strong indication that King David will one day be reunited with that baby for eternity. But until then, he must press on.

We live in such a broken world, and we groan for the day when there is no more brokenness. The good news is, that will come one day.

This is good news for those who come to recognize that Jesus is the Son of God, and that he's come to save us. It's good news for those who recognize that Jesus really is our only hope and that he is the one who bridges the wide gap between our sin's consequence (which is death) and a holy and righteous God, who can provide life eternal.

The final takeaway concerning King David's story here is that none of us deserves the mercy and grace of God. He understood this.

You can see this throughout all the Psalms that he writes. He recognizes that he is born in sin and will die a sinner and the wages of sin is death. But Jesus has come to provide life.

That's how much God loves you. If you've been told anything else, it's false.

When we're going through a period in life following a bad decision, we must understand that if we bring our confession to God and are a child of Him, there is no more condemnation. Condemnation comes from the enemy, and this is why many people suffer intense depression. It's because they've believed the lies of the enemy and allowed those lies to define them.

Look at what Paul writes in Romans 8:1: "So now there is no condemnation for those who belong to Christ Jesus."

You need to understand that Jesus died for you once and for all. Will we have to deal with the effects and consequences of our sin here on earth? Yes. But when we understand that our status as adopted sons and daughters of God doesn't get canceled out due to our sin, our minds can become set free.

Much of our depression comes from thoughts that define us that don't originate from God. Think about it: you sin and you believe you are worthless. Where can we find this in the Bible?

I believe that the devil loves depression. He loves to speak lies. He loves to keep kicking you when you're on the ground. The devil kicks you. Jesus extends his hands to lift you.

So, friend, bring all that's on your mind to Jesus. Jesus says, "Come to me, all of you who are weary and carry heavy burdens, and I will give you rest."

Depression is too heavy of a burden to carry. We must stop believing that Jesus has given up on us. He hasn't. He comes back every day and knocks on your door until you answer.

For the church, we must make our spaces places where confession can take place and restoration can happen. But so often, churches don't have these places. Restoration must be a gentle process because it is how Jesus would operate.

Let our churches be places where people can come and bring their burdens and heaviness. Let us also know that we are no better than the people that bring their burdens and heaviness. No, it can happen to anyone, including you and me.

How do I know that? Jeremiah 17:9 says, "The human heart is the most deceitful of all things, and desperately wicked. Who really knows how bad it is?"

No one is immune from doing stupid things in life, and we need to stop thinking we are. No one is immune from the emotional fall-out that comes from doing stupid things, so let's be a little bit more compassionate, especially to those who desire to be restored.

We must not put anyone on a pedestal. When we do this, we are seeing them for who we want them to be and what you want to see instead of who they really are. As a pastor, I always tell people to just call me by my first name. I get it, though. There's a responsibility that comes from pastoring, but I am in the same boat as the average Joe. I'm broken just like you. I'm not better than you, and I don't desire to be. We are all sinners in need of God's crazy grace.

Every day, I recognize that I am so blessed. With all that God has brought me through, I am so fortunate to have all that I have. Even in those periodic seasons of depression, I rely on the grace and strength of God to minister to me through it all because I remember what He has done for me. God loved me at my worst, and the same is true for you.

Paul writes, in Romans 5:8, "But God showed his great love for us by sending Christ to die for us while we were still sinners." Isn't that amazing? He died for us at our worst; not when we got our house in order. I continue to be stunned by this.

ABOUT THE AUTHOR

After growing up being tossed around the foster care system, Bryan is now a successful graduate of Gordon College and Southwestern Baptist Theological Seminary. With a strong passion for discipleship and outreach, Bryan pastors an urban campus at one of New England's largest churches. He, his wife, and his five kids love all things water-related and are passionate advocates for good pizza.

Printed in the USA
CPSIA information can be obtained
at www.ICGtesting.com
LVHW041042200824
788522LV00002B/9